DRIVING
DIGITAL
TRANSFORMATION

Reshape the Future of your Business

Includes More than *51 Practical Examples*

DRIVING DIGITAL TRANSFORMATION

Reshape the Future of your Business

Includes More than *51 Practical Examples*

RAKTIM SINGH

Published Internationally by

Pendown Press

Powered by G **Gullybaba**

PENDOWN PRESS

Powered by **Gullybaba Publishing House Pvt. Ltd.,**
An ISO 9001 & ISO 14001 Certified Co.,
Regd. Office: 2525/193, 1st Floor, Onkar Nagar-A, Tri Nagar,
Delhi-110035
Ph.: 09350849407, 09312235086
E-mail: info@pendownpress.com
Branch Office: 1A/2A, 20, Hari Sadan, Ansari Road,
Daryaganj, New Delhi-110002
Ph.: 011-45794768
Website: PendownPress.com

First Edition: 2021
Price: ₹399/-
ISBN: 978-93-90557-28-8

CONTENTS

REVIEWS

"As an industry leader engaged with digital transformation, Raktim Singh has shared his rich experience through this book. This a very interesting read, as the industry is undergoing a major transformation, where mindset change and technological change have to meld together for business continuity and growth."

Dr S. Raghunath
Chairperson, Centre For Corporate Governance and Citizenship Professor of Strategy IIM Bangalore Bannerghatta Road Bangalore INDIA

"Here is a much-awaited book on a subject, which is much talked about but little understood.

Based on his rich experience of bringing about digital transformation in several traditional industries, Raktim has shared the necessary ingredients and the secret recipe for business transformation in this fascinating book, which would well prepare the readers to transform their own businesses for the digital world.

Reading this book made me pause on several occasions and reflect on what I need to do in my own organization.

Anyone who is serious about preparing his organization for the Digital World cannot afford to miss reading this fascinating book!"

Vinaya Varma
MD & CEO Mjunction Services Limited

"This book is a great practical guide for understanding the digital transformation. It helps the reader understand topics of current technology and their role in driving digitalization. This is recommended as 'essential- reading' for all those who wish to understand the current trends and the application of these technologies to drive transformation."

Chinmay Trivedi
Treasurer, GE Healthcare Chicago, IL, USA

"An engaging book simplified by an experienced techie. His industry experience clearly shows the way to the leaders and executives as to how to achieve true Digital Transformation by various tips and tricks. His in-depth knowledge of technology makes it evident that we have much more potential to revolutionize the industry by being more flexible in adopting the technology. A must-read and good going Raktim Singh!"

Tridibesh Satpathy,
CEO, VMEdu Inc and Lead Author of the Scrum Body of Knowledge
(SBOK Guide)

"An engaging and a practical handbook designed for leaders and executives who wish to understand the opportunities offered by true Digital Transformation and embark on their own transformation journey. A must-read and good going Raktim Singh!"

Anil Kanitkar
Programme Manager Singapore

"A much-awaited book on having a varied range of aspects on digital transformation thoughts with rich corporate research showcasing technology indicators of future work and the overall transformation of the industry is quite insightful. Completely agree with transformational thoughts."

Himanshu Paliwal
Vice President at Bank of America-Emerging Data Platforms
(Data Science and ML) at Bank of America Edison,
New Jersey, United States

"The book is based on good research study about future technology and solutions in a very thoughtful way. Raktim Singh does a great job of explaining core fundamental aspects of being digital, what and how part in a very simplistic way!"

Atul Kumar
CEO, 110 Allen Rd, Basking Ridge, NJ 07920
www.cliksource.com

"An exceptional book to understand the increased relevance of fast-paced Digital Transformation in the post-COVID era."

Pankaj Kumar Singh,
Indian Revenue Service (IRS)

"This book is a must-read for leaders and executives who have a game-plan for moving their businesses into the digital era and need to reinforce their strategies with first-hand, fresh and uniquely potent ideas. The author has extensive transformation experience along with deep domain and technology expertise, which is evident as you read through the numerous examples that span personal to professional to social milieus. Some of the ground-breaking insights are in the references to digital anthropology -ground-breaking because the simple and lucid depictions might just be the catalyst for change that complex transformations are in most need of."

Rintu Patnaik
Sr Director, RI/P&C Insurance (APAC EMEA),
Sapiens India

"The Book Digital Transformation covers a lot of topics on future technology like AI/IoT/Cloud/Data and their role in making digitally transformed industries of our times. Good research and methodology to explain their interrelationships. Highly recommended!"

Manoj Khatri
Director, Project and Infrastructure Finance
A Leading International Bank

"This book highlights the transformational age in which we are living in and how pioneer companies are leading the digital disruption of business models. The author has a good grasp of all the technologies involved and extensive experience of working on such transformational initiatives. The various frameworks, case studies and examples discussed will be useful for many executives or leaders who are looking to apply these concepts."

Vishal Agarwal
Partner-Consulting
Ernst & Young

ABOUT THE AUTHOR

Raktim Singh, as he describes himself, is "one of the few lucky software professionals, who are Software Product Native". From day one, Raktim got the opportunity to work in Infosys' FINACLE suite of products.

He has done his B.TECH from IIT-BHU and joined Infosys, FINACLE in 1995.

He had implemented Agile & DevOps practices in various FINACLE products. He is a certified SAFe 4.0 (Scaled Agile Framework) Agilist.

During his 25 years at Infosys FINACLE, he had developed many products in Wealth Management & Corporate Banking domain.

Raktim is a digital enthusiast and blogger. His blogs related to Digital transformation had been published on various social media platforms.

Raktim is an avid book reader and has a personal library of more than 600 books.

He also mentors IIM graduates on software product principles. He is part of international Toastmaster Club and has won many awards there. Raktim is also a member of India FIN-TECH & Bangalore FIN-TECH group.

You can reach to Raktim by these social medial links:

@dadraktim

www.raktimsingh.com

http://linkedin.com/in/raktim-singh-b7127513a

https://instagram.com/raktim938?igshid=1xtcjpgw16e1e

PREFACE

This is DECEMBER 2020. We are already more than nine months into COVID-19. A year back, no one would have imagined a situation like this. Many companies (based on their business type and digital preparedness)have survived while many companies are at the brink of bankruptcy.

If your business was not really close to the customers, you and your company must have surely faced some hardships. On the up-side, the sales of high-end laptops, mobiles and tablets have gone up and almost every home is rushing to install Wi-Fi (if it was not already done).

Companies, whose services or products a customer can avail by sitting at home, are seeing an uptick in their business. On similar lines, companies, where their employees can work from home or anyplace, are continuing production. This is what I call "Customer to Business". We can face more situations like these in the coming days.

This is not the last crisis humanity has faced, and technology has come to aid to keep things going on in such a grim environment. Instead of just sitting back and waiting for a miracle, we have to make efforts to reach a stage where we can map the uncertainties of the future and leverage the right technology for our best possible use.

The last decade has gone through a drastic transformation in business models across the world. The business world no longer operates on the traditional methods, and all the major organizations have already seen significant disruptions in their models. This disruption is attributed to Digital Transformation across all layers of organizations as well as our personal lives.

We live in an age of instant gratification, virtualization and hyper-personalization when it comes to consuming the maximum number of services around us. These things happened due to the advent of certain technologies; they have changed the equations of businesses all across the world. The examples of this transformation are FAAAN companies-Facebook, Amazon, Apple, Alphabet and Netflix.

While these organizations have showcased how to lead digitally and capture a major market share, many across the world have adopted this transformation only on a superficial level. They are still grappling with the age-old challenges.

I have explained those reasons in this book, what acts as a roadblock and what makes a mindset and organizational transformation in a digital way.

As an IT professional for over 25 years with one of the leading IT firms of the country, it was a privilege to witness digital transformation at hand. Sharing those ground realities of the journey of Digital Transformation is the essence of this book.

I hope my efforts shed-adequate light on this revolutionary process happening all around us and help you in solving the puzzle to a considerable extent.

MESSAGE
FROM DISRUPTOR

Dear Reader,

I am a DISRUPTOR, who keeps appearing in every decade. For more than four centuries, you and your forefathers must have felt my impact. I have changed the way you travel, the way you talk with each other, the way you light your house… the way you connect to others.

In year 2020, I came in the form of COVID-19!

You can't avoid me. I have many avatars. But by reading this book, you can prepare yourself better to handle me.

Let me share a small story.

This story dates back to the time when Einstein was a teacher. One day, during an exam, he distributed question papers to his students. To everyone's surprise, the paper had the same questions from the previous year. Einstein's assistant asked him, "Why are the questions the same as last year?"

He thought for a moment and replied: "Yes, they are same. But this year, the answers are different."

The same is true for your business. In case of disruption, you should know:

1. How to continue providing more value to your customers and keep increasing your profits too?

2. How to reduce cost?

3. How to capture new markets and customers?

But the answers to these eternal questions keep changing every year.

Raktim has done a good job in providing answers. Read this carefully if you want to handle me.

Yours truly,

DISRUPTOR

FOREWORD

Digital and Digitization have been the biggest opportunity and challenge for businesses all over the globe. They have disrupted established businesses like never before in history. It is quite evident in the churn that has taken place in the S&P, most-valued company for the last 15 years. What used to be dominated by Citi, Exxon, GM, GE, Walmart and other brick and mortar companies have given ways to Apple, Amazon, Alphabet, Microsoft. The top eight most-valued organizations in that list are platform companies, which are helping digital transformation on a population scale.

Keeping this as the central theme, Raktim has brought out all his experience in this book advocating Digital as the means to business transformation. He has emphasized on the importance and necessity of going digital to achieve the business transformation in a layman's language, such that business leaders' world should be able to get a few ideas for them to go ahead with much needed digital transformation.

While describing the current scenario, and analyzing the most successful corporations globally, Raktim has curated very important and strategic suggestions that are practical and implementable by businesses world over. By not limiting the book to a specific region or industry, Raktim has brought out a simple yet comprehensive framework for digital adoption for business transformation.

By going through the content, one can easily come to the conclusion that the book is an outcome of a practitioner's insights distilled for over 25 years to help practitioners in their journey of digitization and business transformation.

In this book, Raktim stresses on the institutionalization of the framework, industrialization of experiences, instrumentation of processes, the democratization of IT and consumerization of Enterprise Apps, thereby, providing the much-needed impetus for a structural way to digitally transforming global businesses.

For the readers of this book, the key takeaway is the ACID Framework that Raktim passionately explains in four sections. ACID (AI, Cloud, IoT, Data), which is quintessential pillars of any Digital Transformation has been explained with hand-picked practical case studies from across multiple industries.

Finally, Raktim elevates the entire conversation on how to keep organizations alive and up-to-date by investing in continuous learning, being agile and leveraging the power of networking, eco-system and partnerships.

As a bonus, for the readers, Raktim has also curated best of his Linked-in postings on this topic. I'm certain that this book is going to help all the digital practitioners and aspiring business transformation leaders as a quick guide and checklist for them to achieve success in a proven and practical way.

I thank Raktim for this opportunity, and I wish to see him publish many more papers and books that capture his practical experience, and also insights.

Rajashekara Visweswara Maiya
VP, Global Head-Business Consulting-Finacle
at Infosys Bangalore Urban, Karnataka, India

ACKNOWLEDGEMENT

Discussion with Sai!

Sai: Raktim, this fourth industrial revolution is quite different. It seems everyone will lose jobs.

Me: We have always heard similar misconceptions before each revolution, Sai. As per my understanding, before motor cars were launched, everyone said that human beings would become jobless. But I think only horses lost jobs! Horse cart owners learnt car driving and got a new type of job.

Sai: Software will consume the world. Other revolutions were different.

Me: Okay. Let me explore and learn.

To get the right answer, I started to interact with various industry leaders, attend webinars and read books. And then, in March 2020, the COVID-19 disruption happened. Within six months, the pandemic forced and facilitated all of us to start living the 'new normal'. We all have started doing many things, which were considered unthinkable in the past (working from home, not venturing out). It has also helped me to understand the power of digital technology.

This book is the culmination of all my learnings in the above context.

I keep telling my friends about the conversation I and Sai had.

One day, one of my friends asked– "Raktim, Who is 'Sai'?" And I answered– "Sai is inside my heart, mind... and the Superpower."

Before I begin, I want to seek blessings from:

1. My parents, Sri Rajpal Singh and Smt. Krishna, my uncle Sri Hirday Narayan Agarwal and Aunt Smt. Nirmala Agarwal.

2. My mentors-Suresh Padmanabhan Sir, Divya Shlokam & Bhuwan Pant.

3. My son, Rishith, who watches all tech events live (Apple Developer Conference, Samsung Unpacked, Google Launch NightIn) and asks difficult questions. My lovely daughter Deveshi, who asks me after each event, "Why can't we buy that new gadget (phone, watch, tablet, smart light...)?" And thanks to my wife Ratna, who has always supported me in all my endeavors.

4. Thanks to my brother Rajat, for all his love and affection.

CHAPTER 1

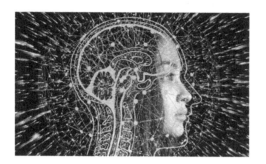

DIGITAL TRANSFORMATION AN INTRODUCTION

"The next five years will be more disruptive than the last 15. This is NOT business as usual. A lot of technology that came in three years ago doesn't work anymore."

–Jeremy Waite

B usiness is not the way it was a decade ago. The working style and process have changed a lot. This credit apparently goes to the term- Digital Transformation. Talking about Artificial Intelligence and Cloud Technology, it looks trendy when we boast of doing business in digital ways. Our personal lives have also shown a change in some important habits and we, proudly, declare ourselves as 'digitally transformed'.

Digital transformation, with the modern tools and processes, are collated to solve business problems and charter new paths of innovations in work-life situations.

The way in which we think, talk and work are different today. I remember there were times when we had to buy groceries, we would visit the nearby store, see the items, touch them and feel their freshness and then buy it. Today, in the digital era, we scroll our mobile screens, add to cart, and place an order; almost everything is available online. Even at 6 am, you just wake up to find these delivery persons at your doorstep!

This transformation is visible to us in every aspect of life- be it buying groceries, reading books, watching movies or ordering exotic cuisines from our favorite restaurant. We just need to log in to the respective brand portal and access the service.

It didn't evolve in a 'swoosh' or an 'abracadabra' way. This transformational process has taken several years for the business leaders and common people to assimilate the digital ways of thinking and put their trust behind the new technology.

Whether or not we like these changes, the disruption has happened and it is here to stay. Those who followed the footsteps of changes are leading with examples as to what a true digital transformation can offer as perks of life. Companies like Facebook, Amazon, Apple, Alphabet and Netflix have disrupted their own models, time and again, and are marching ahead through a new century like a pro.

As against this, there is a huge population out there, which is still skeptical of this change and lying either in the transitional stage of transformation or just starting the process. Both these groups still refer to themselves as 'digitally transformed' and are not able to get their acts together.

Most of the organizations today call themselves 'Digitally Transformed'. It's common to hear businesses say that they are 'Agile' and have shifted their entire operations to the cloud, and other such things, but when we dig a little deeper, we find, many people's mindset is still stuck to the traditional ways. We are still struggling to break multiple silos in our system & trying hard to come out of old habits. The transformation happened, but superficially.

Mentally and culturally, many are still in the same phase. As a result of which, there are a lot of problems in the layers of these organizations. I have seen managers hating processes like Agile. The reason is not the technology but the old mindset that refuses to transform. As a result of this, the hiring managers and the new recruits find themselves in a conflicting space with the management. The ideation dies with friction from the top-level leadership.

I have put my best foot forward in explaining, through this book, what makes a business truly digital, who are the leaders of this revolution and what factors of technology truly transform your ways of working.

The first two chapters talk about the real meaning of digital transformation. Is it just the adoption of a certain technology that makes us digital or do we need to dive deeper into the layers of our society and consider tracing the genesis of transformation?

What are the features and challenges that prevent the holistic assimilation of technological transformation in our lifestyle and business?

This is followed by knowing the four pillars of Digital Transformation- ACID, *i.e.* Artificial Intelligence (AI), Cloud, Internet of Things (IoT), and Data, which has led to this revolution. These four technologies have changed the entire landscape of business operations and consumption of services over the last decade.

The sections following this explore how these technologies have invoked our subconscious mind and transformed our thoughts and beliefs. Digital Anthropology is close to my heart and I have detailed out, how deeper knowledge of Digital Anthropology, will help us in sustaining this transformation. To make this transformation, future proof, understanding of Digital Anthropology is very important.

Technology has crept into our lives in such a way that it has led to drug-like addictions. It has both negative and positive impacts. In true sense, today, technology knows much more about us than anyone else, thanks to AI (Artificial Intelligence) & Internet of Things.

The final section of the book conveys my thoughts about digital transformation around us; I keep sharing them on LinkedIn with my professional networks, along with the Frequently Asked Questions from the readers. As an IT professional, I have seen these changes closely and, so, I've tried to explain it in the simplest possible ways.

Final Words

Digital Transformation is not just about the tools, technology and processes; it is a holistic process, which starts right from having a "Right mindset'. Once you figure out the cultural issues of your organization & decide to solve them, the process of transformation becomes smooth. The entire chain of the business process should benefit from the transformation, including the suppliers, vendors, employees and consumers. It's a holistic process of unlearning the old lessons and learning the new things, which might take years or decades, but it starts from you right now. The sooner we accept the disruptions, the better we can accommodate the future of innovations.

As they say- old ways of thinking never bring new changes. Let's begin the transformation from the mental level first to see its physical manifestations.

Ready? Dive further!

CHAPTER 2

WHAT IS DIGITAL TRANSFORMATION?

In my opinion, we need to separate digital and transformation. You must go through business or personal transformation to achieve digital experience. The transformation is all about adapting the digital experience in business and personal fronts.

Digital experience is not about the Internet, channels, Mobile APPS or e-commerce alone. That is more like lipstick on the pig. This was the mistake done by many companies earlier.

Many companies thought that if they have a website and offer their products on mobiles also, they are digital-ready. That's not the case!

You just can't have one Chief Digital Officer and a 'cool technology team' to really transform your organization. As I said, you need to think and overhaul, both "Outside In and Inside Out".

Digital experience, according to me, is a process wherein 'WHAT' we are doing remains the same, but the difference lies in 'HOW' we do it... Digital channels, as a medium, provide us with the same services but with a different approach. The service requirement is the same, but the ways of consuming those services have changed a lot. The 'What' of things have remained the same, but the 'How' of things have changed. For example, I don't have to step out of my home to buy groceries, shop for clothes and accessories or book a travel ticket. I can get all these from the comfort of my home with a few clicks on my smartphone or laptop. In simple words, services are in the hands of the customers now.

When the digital experience traverses the factors of anytime, place and device, digital transformation gets in complete sync with the layers around us and becomes a part of our lifestyle. The strategy of digital experience is not driven by the IT world alone, it's the customer needs that plays a major role. There is a great difference between simply taking advantage of new technology and actually utilizing it to enhance user experiences and better address their needs. This is in a real sense called 'digital experience'.

To understand the concept better, let us distinguish between what is 'DIGITAL Experience' and how to do business transformation with the help of new technologies.

Digital transformation consists of four aspects:

1. Understanding the true meaning of digital experience
2. Understanding the cultural mindset & ground realties of your organization. (Refer Chapter-3 for this)
3. Understanding new technologies & using them properly to transform the business process around us. (Chapter-5 to 8 covers this)
4. Understanding Digital Anthropology, so as to change your mindset & subconscious mind. This will help

you in making sure that you are able to sustain this transformation journey in future. (Chapter-9 to 11 covers this)

Please note that out of four aspects, technology is only one of them. Technology is "ONLY" an enabler. Also, tomorrow some other technology will come. You have to pay equal attention to the other three aspects to really drive this digital transformation journey & be well prepared to sustain this in future.

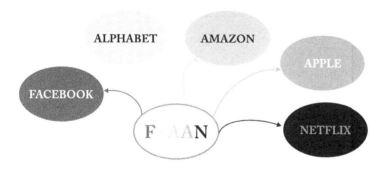

Digital Experience championed by FAAAN Companies

The FAAAN companies around us have best demonstrated this digital experience. By FAAAN companies, we mean the five major organizations, which have changed the entire landscape of digital experience. They are:

- Facebook started in 2004
- Amazon started in 1994
- Apple started in 1976
- Google stated in 1998 and Alphabet started in 2015
- Netflix stated in 1997

These companies, over time, have demonstrated that even if the 'WHAT' has remained the same, the 'HOW' of the entire service consumption pattern can be changed for better results.

Although we are witnessing metamorphosis in almost every sector now, these were the companies that brought a revolutionary change in our mindset and gave us a good taste of Digital experience. Moving ahead, we will see a glimpse of how these pioneer organizations work and how they have managed to keep the customers engaged in an ever-changing digital world; they have been giving the best experiences that are simply wonderful.

Facebook

We are social animals; it is a general human trait. The inherent need to interact with other humans is primitive. Earlier, we socialized with people physically in our social and professional circles. We had a close group of people with whom we shared our lifestyle choices, flaunted our clothes, jewelry, lifestyle and whatnot.

We are still doing them but little differently now. All our social interactions have now moved to online platforms. We have an online group of known and unknown people who form our so-called 'Friends' circle. These are the people whom we may know, or we may not know. The definition of 'close group' has changed in our 'dictionaries'. We publish stories, photos, selfies, food preferences, clothes we newly bought, give a tour of our houses, luxury cars, jobs, promotions, colleagues, achievements and celebrations on the online platform without any inhibitions. Just like our real lives, we compete with each other on Facebook to flaunt all our goodies and try to create a 'mini-celebrity' status for ourselves where everything looks flawless.

Didn't we do the same in front of our social circle, earlier? Do you get that? The '**How**' may have changed but the '**What**' is still the same! Facebook has changed our ways of interactions completely, and we aren't getting enough of it.

Apple

Every possible experience that involves reading, listening to music, talking, clicking pictures, biometric scanning and movie watching -all these have been transformed since the time APPLE arrived. Every new product of APPLE introduces us to a new magical feature.

Apple reshaped the future of the music industry when it brought the concept of iPod and disrupted the entire CD experience. The music industry went digital in no time, and ever since, we have seen Apple disrupting its own models by its innovations and changing the 'HOW' model of the industry, innovating the 'WHAT' for a smoother experience. This kind of transformation has completely reshaped our digital experiences.

Apple surely makes things taste delicious with its newer digital experiences, and we are not complaining!

Amazon

Amazon has been a trend setter in the digital world. Be it shopping for grocery, clothing, home products, kitchenware, buying books or watching movies, Amazon has brought the market to our doorsteps in just one click! The deliveries are as safe and secure just like the conventional, offline shopping experience. We don't have to depend on the store timings. We are free to shop at any odd hour of the day, or shall I say even at night? Of late, Amazon has even claimed to deliver at doorstep via its drone services within two hours!

We are still shopping for the same things and paying the sellers, but the mode has changed. The only difference is we order things online via our phones or laptops and pay through credit cards, e-wallets or debit cards. The service has become faster and better. So, this entire digital experience has kept our 'WHAT' same and 'HOW' different.

Alphabet

Alphabet, the parent company of Google, has transformed the way in which we search for anything online; I am talking about Google Search. We can now search for any physical location, online through Google Maps, how the internet reaches remote places (Google Fibre & Loon),how the mind of machine works (Deep Mind), and do much more. 'Google' has already become a verb now. We don't search anymore, we Google it!

Netflix

When Netflix arrived in 1997, none of us could have imagined, even in our wildest of dreams, lying on our home couch having homemade popcorn and binge-watching movies in a cost-effective, yet flexible way. Today, Netflix has brought us to times, wherein watching movies on-demand from the comforts of our home is happening in real-time, and it looks so natural, even though it has actually changed. All that we need to do is log in to Netflix and start watching from the extensive range of movie choices. If we don't like a movie, we can instantly switch to another one with zero friction. In simple words, video streaming is happening in real-time.

I would like to reiterate there is no change in our interest in watching movies. We still wait for weekends or late nights to get a break from the daily routines. We no longer have to worry about booking a ticket at a theatre in advance, moving out of cozy homes and travel long distances to watch our favorite movies. We can watch them at the desired time and according to our own taste and preferred place. Everything else has changed except the 'WHAT' of the movie experience. The 'HOW' defines the lifestyle brought about by the digital experience gifted to us by Netflix.

Digital Experience in the Music and Movie

• The Music Experience

Music has been a stress buster for many people. There was a time when we had cassette tapes to listen to our favorite music, and then came the era of CDs, Mini Discs, Vinyl records, iPods and MP3s. Today, music, including radio, is streamed online. The way of listening to music is completely digitized.

The 'What'- *i.e.* the music is still the same, but the way of consumption of music has transformed a lot over time. The experience of listening to music has become digital now.

• The Movie Experience

Just like the transformation that music has gone through, the 'how' of the movie-watching experience has also changed over time. No one has to wait for the mercy of the cable operators to stream some good movies– we have been tired of watching same old 'Golden 60's' movies on Sundays! Isn't it? The introduction of DVDs had changed the algorithm of watching movies, people could buy or rent them.

Classic Examples of Transformation

The Netflix Story: An Exemplary Story of transformation: Netflix was launched in 1997, at a time when Blockbuster, a movie giant, was the undisputed champion in renting out movie DVDs. Blockbuster had a brick and mortar rental chain with around¬ 2,800 stores across the world during1985-1992. Viacom acquired Blockbuster for $8.4 billion in 1994.

Netflix, soon, entered the business by introducing rental service by mail. Next, the movie streaming giant approached Blockbuster for a merger proposal. It demanded a $50 million for the merger to run the Blockbuster brand online. The deal didn't materialize, and in fact, it was taken so casually by Blockbuster's CEO John Antioco that he almost laughed at the deal during the proposal.

In 1999, Groupe Arnault backed Netflix with $30 million cash to launch a subscription- based service.

In business, you need to tie your profits to what your customers value. But in case of Blockbuster, it was different. Much of their profit relied on something their customers despised–late fees.

With Netflix, customers could keep the DVDs as long as they wanted so there were no late fees–ever.

Internet Source: : 3 Facts About the Blockbuster Netflix Story You Probably Didn't Know (disruptdaily.com).

Think about it, a huge portion of the revenue Blockbuster needed to stay in business was a revenue stream Netflix didn't even have.

When consumers heard Netflix's original ad campaign, "The end of late fees," Blockbuster heard a death knell.

In 2004, Blockbuster, too, launched an online platform like Netflix for its services and managed to get 2 million subscribers by 2006. But, Netflix had grown to 6.3 million subscribers by then! Netflix soon signed a deal with Straz to stream 1,000 blockbuster movies on its online platform. In 2010, Netflix signed the deal with giants like Sony, Paramount, Lions gate and Disney for 20 per cent viewership share for North America audience.

By this time, the fate of Blockbuster was sealed, and it was delisted from the New York Stock Exchange in 2010, and it, finally, filed for bankruptcy having $1 billion losses.

Netflix's valuation at that time was $24 million. Today, it has increased to $203 billion, which is a spectacular increase of 4060%!

The incredible transformation that Netflix went through was such that it disrupted their business model, twice! First, their model was based on rent-a-DVD, which then changed to streaming movies online. Currently, they have moved from streaming other producers' movie to their in-house production movies and TV shows. The first show created by Netflix was

'House of Cards' in 2013 which was very successful and went on for six seasons.

AMAZON-THE EVERYTHING STORE

Amazon started it's journey in 1994. The company started as an online marketplace for books but expanded to sell electronics, software, video games, apparel, furniture, food, toys, and jewelry.

And now, it's everywhere. We have Amazon e-commerce market place, Amazon Movies, Amazon Web Services, Amazon Prime, Alexa…. Really 'an AMAZONING journey'!!!

Though this journey contains many inspiring & useful examples, I want to quote one related to Amazon API's mandate.

In corporate world, many of us live in a world of PPT (Power Point Presentations). It's a sheer waste of time and energy for both employees and employers. Most people would agree that many times, a shabby work was decorated with beautiful presentation. This hid the major data and operational flaws in the decision-making process.

Amazon took the lead in changing this 'Culture of PPTs'. In around 2002, Jeff Bezos clearly stated a mandate which reflected the true transformational mindset of using digital technology. Jeff Bezos' order came like this:

- All teams will, henceforth, expose their data and functionality through service interfaces.

- The teams must communicate with each other through these interfaces.

- There will be no other form of inter-process communication allowed: no direct linking, no direct reads of another team's data store, no shared-memory model and no back-doors whatsoever. The only communication allowed is via service interface calls over the network.

- It doesn't matter what technology they use. HTTP, Corba, Pubsub, custom protocols—doesn't matter. Bezos doesn't care.

- All service interfaces, without exception, must be designed from the ground up to be externalizable. That is to say, the team must plan and design to be able to expose the interface to developers in the outside world. No exceptions.

- Anyone who doesn't do this will be fired. Thank you; have a nice day!

I want to emphasize that Jeff Bezos issued this in year 2002. For many of us, making presentations through 'Wow' PPT was a cool thing during those times. But visionary Jeff Bezos saw the effort, which get wasted & how real data get hidden below these 'Wow' & 'Cool' PPTs.

This transformation brought a real change in the mindset of the employees at the cultural levels and, hence, assimilated into the deeper layers of the organization.

The Foundations of Digital Experience:

There are many questions that we must answer before we dig deeper into the origins of Digital Experience.

- What are the key aspects of great digital experience, and how do we identify that we have truly achieved and lived the digital experience?

- Is it just the introduction of new technology and the orders of following it blindly without truly appreciating its advent?

- Is it that the new technology has come, everyone has adopted it, and we must adopt it for the sake of looking digitally trendy?

- Shall we adopt it as a trend follower, or shall we genuinely feel that the newer ways of innovation must alter our lifestyles and solve our problems at hand for an easy and efficient lifestyle?

- Are we adopting this new 'cool' digital experience as a solution to our problems, or are we first creating the solutions and then looking for the problems?

To answer these questions, we must be able to find out what features make it a real 'Digital experience'. I feel there are certain features that truly mark the advent of digital experience. They are detailed below:

1. **Digitization Leading to Virtualization**

2. **Instant Gratification**

3. **Flawless Automation leading to Industrialization**

4. **Hyper-Personalization**

Let us understand how each of these factors will help you in achieving the true 'digital experience'.

1. Digitization Leading to Virtualization

By Virtualization, we mean that any data, service or application is available virtually, for example, on the Cloud. To get a true digital experience, any application must have its software-based and virtual representation on a storage place like Cloud. Here, we create the virtual version of an application.

If we look at the history of Virtualization, it began in 1960 to divide the system resource provided by mainframe computers between different applications.

Virtualization has its benefits in terms of efficiency and cost-effectiveness. Data centre management becomes simple, along with an improvement in the efficiency, agility and responsiveness. The downtime is considerably reduced in the case of Operating System and application crash. Multiple redundant machines can run alongside if such a problem arises; it is cost- effective as compared to the physical servers.

Virtualization makes it much more time-efficient to configure and install an application. These virtual machines run applications faster. Hence, it is easier to automate and assimilate them in present work flows.

Our daily activities & hobbies

It's amazing to see that most of our habits like reading newspaper or books, listening to music, watching movies, etc., have been slowly transforming with Virtualization. We no longer have to visit those exclusive stores to purchase books as they are available on multiple platforms like Kindle, Kobo and Play Store. In the pandemic era, we saw many people switching to e-Reading.

Music is, now, available on platforms like Spotify and iTunes rather than the age-old cassettes and CDs. Watching movies have also shifted to online streaming as against the conventional ways of going to theatres or watching on televisions. So, practically the whole world is moving towards Virtualization as far as technology is concerned.

Office Emails

Many of us must have got access to office email facility around 1990. But, there were two major limitations to this:

- We were allowed/given a limited size to store emails. After the mailboxes reached that size, we were asked to delete large-size emails.

- Accessing those emails (or for that matter, any other office application) outside the office network was cumbersome. We were given hardware secure cards to generate random pin. One had to use that to login to email and other official applications.

I am assuming that as of today, your office email must have been put on CLOUD (by taking advantage of virtualization).

There's no size limitation for office emails anymore. On similar notes, accessing those official emails, outside the office, has turned out to be very easy.

For many of us it was a relief while working from home during COVID-19 lockdown, and the pandemic restrictions; I am able to access all official applications, very smoothly.

2. The Flawless Automation -Industrialization

The Industrialization has helped in making sure that the items ordered, reach the right place safely and with zero friction in procuring it. A perfect example of this is the online grocery procurement. We can order groceries from anywhere at any time nowadays. We are no longer dependent on the opening or closing times of the grocery stores; we can instantly order and receive the same in the minimum possible time. Amazon claims that its drone services can deliver groceries in less than two hours at specific locations.

In India, Mumbai Dabbawalla is the perfect example of Industrialization. Dabbawallas (also called Tiffin wallahs) constitute a lunchbox delivery and return system. They collect hot lunch boxes from homes and restaurants and deliver them at the given location in Mumbai. The delivery team picks up lunchboxes of their customers by late morning, travel through bicycles or trains as the modes of transport to deliver the same to the given location and return the empty boxes in the afternoon. The model runs flawless like an industrialized model.

3. Instant Gratification

Real digital experience should give instant gratification to it's users. Instant gratification is a big differentiator in this. According to a massive study from UMass Amherst, which surveyed 6.7 million users, it was predicted 'the viewers tend to abandon online videos if they take more than 2 seconds to load'.

In this age, when the attention span of people has reduced to a mere 5-minute video length, there is a huge demand for technology to give instant output. This is now getting manifested in most of the activities. Be it ordering groceries online, watching movies, downloading videos or anything else, we want instant services.

There was a time when I wished to watch a movie, I had to pre-book the tickets and then go to the theatre. It was not an easy task to reach the movie theatre, especially in metro cities like Bengaluru and Mumbai, where traffic crawls at snail's pace. After the advent of OTT platforms, watching movies is as seamless as calling a near one over the phone. So, instant gratification is one of the key features of digital experience.

Netflix gives us this amazing experience of watching our favorite movies from the comforts of our cozy homes. We can search, pause, rewind or fast forward the movie as per our requirement. We just need to log in for the movie service to be available immediately. There is zero friction in accessing the movie-watching experience.

With Kindle: Before COVID, I used to travel a lot and attend various conference & seminars in various cities. When you are in a new city, it's difficult to find & travel to a book store in that city. At-least for me, KINDLE had solved this problem. Irrespective of the city, I can always download a book on my kindle. And yes, during travel, my luggage weight has come down. No need to carry 10 physical books to read during travel time. One Kindle is enough.

4. Hyper-Personalization

Hyper-personalization is another important feature of digital experience. With inbuilt Artificial Intelligence in today's products, there is a trace of personalization in every service that is delivered at our doorstep. The more personalized the service is, the more transformational digital experience will be.

Have you ever seen the text reading 'recommended for you', 'people you may know also bought this', 'you may also like', etc., while searching for a product online?

Based on your orders and personal preferences, similar options flash before you. Does AI have something to do with these recommendations?

Yes, you are right! AI has mapped your choices. It knows you much better and suggests the products, which closely reflect your choices.

The books, groceries, movies, online videos, gifts are all personalized with the induction of AI technology.

Netflix displays movie and show recommendations based on our previous watching habits and also depending on what is popular in our country. The movie streaming giant most likely identified that users seek recommendations from their friends before deciding which movie or show to watch next. So, it has introduced this feature. In the present model, Netflix recommends movies and shows based on various parameters like:

1. Global popularity (Popular on Netflix)

2. National popularity (Top 10 in India Today or US Today)

3. User's viewing preferences (For example you watched Black Mirror)

4. Netflix Originals...

In my opinion, the second parameter (National popularity) was introduced recently. Many a times, people in a country want to know, what their friends/relatives are watching. Now this parameter helps a person in knowing which all movies are popular/trending in his country/social circle.

I think, this provides a good incentive to a person, to watch those movie (popular in his country).

Disneyland and Customer Care

Disneyland has also adopted a similar model where it looked into customer issues and solved the problems using digital ways. When we visit any Disneyland park, we can install their app and book a slot for rides using it.

This app gives access to updated data like the kind of ride (whether it is a wet or dry ride, thrilling ride or roller-coaster, etc.), wait time and maintenance updates for various rides. Disneyland parks are generally situated in a vast area spanning several acres together. So, it's good for visitors to know all the details in advance. We can also book a ride beforehand for a specific time.

In some Disney hotels, we can check-out and hand the luggage to the hotel staff. They will take the flight details and make sure that the luggage is checked into our flights. We don't have to carry it to the airport. Checkout from a Disney Hotel in a relaxed way and their bus will take us to the airport.

This feature of hyper-personalization is now one of the characteristics of this Digital experience.

Final Words

In a nutshell, all these four features - Virtualization, Industrialization, Instant Gratification and Hyper-Personalization make digital experience a truly live able experience. These examples clearly show that if you want to emerge as an industry leader then you have to bring your business near the customer.

Customers will not come to your business, you have to move your business near the customers (& sometimes, literally even in the hands of customer… by smartphones/smartwatch/tablets..)

Tap the nerve of this inquisitive customer, then give them the best digital experience; learn from the leaders. The FAAAN companies have cracked the code of consumer behaviour with their research and innovation, and are now spreading across every nook and corner of the world. These companies have reached the shores of the nations, where these services would not have been able to reach through their mere physical presence. Today, they are present both in the online and offline space. The offline space seems to be fast merging into the online space and the consumers can gain the best of both the worlds.

This "Digital Experience" has once again reinforced the theory: Customer Is The King.

It's time to move your business near The King.

CHAPTER 3

GROUND CHALLENGES IN DIGITAL TRANSFORMATION

Wiki defines Digital Transformation as 'the adoption of digital technology to transform services or businesses through replacing non-digital or manual processes with digital processes or replacing older digital technology with newer digital technology'.

As we start exploring the pathway to digital transformation, we discover that we have to face some challenges along the way to a successful transition. Unless and until these ground challenges are addressed, any kind of technological transformation is difficult in its entirety. To make the most out of the benefits of any technology, the transformation must take place in all its landscapes. Let us have a look at the four challenges, which we may face during this transition process.

Here it is; I call them WISE:

- (W)hy: Know the 'Why' of Your Business
- (I)ntegration with the External World

- (**S**)ilos: Breaking All Kinds of Silos
- (**E**)nvironment and Culture

Let us look at all the above mentioned ground challenges that hamper the success of this holistic transformation.

If we achieve the integration on all these four levels of any organization or society per se, we will experience a complete digital transformation.

1. The Sense of 'Why'

It is very important to figure out the Why of any business for the holistic implementation of Digital Transformation. The 'Why' of the business will define the broader vision of the company.

Let us take a few examples to understand how the knowledge of Why in the business is important for identifying the correct solution for our customer's problems.

The Uber Case: The Ground-Breaking Business Model

Uber, as we know, is one of the most popular car rental services. The customers are aware in advance about the When part of the travel and How much to pay by their Rental Ride Services. Uber's business model has disrupted the traditional car rental services.

It has been seen in many aspects that Uber is providing not just car rental services but also holistic solutions like cost-effective luxurious travel experience.

Uber has tied up with local transport authorities in many countries and cities. In these cities, the Uber App guides which transport mode must be taken to save money on travel. In some cities, the app also provides details of the local train/bus if that is better/faster and nearer to the travelers. Uber, now, helps customers to plan their end-to-end travel by including an additional first mile and last-mile options.

Here, we can see that Uber has figured out its Why, *i.e.* holistic travel solutions. The Why of Uber's business is not limited to providing just car rental services but also support its customers with 'travel-easy' solutions. So, the Why of Uber is travel solution and to become a one-stop-shop for TRAVEL, which has led them to disrupt their business models over time.

The Banking Case: Innovative and Holistic Service Providers
I still remember my childhood, which was spent in a small city. In that city, only three banks were there.

Only one bank was there, near our house. The manager of that bank knew about each and every family member in that locality. He was our 'Bank Uncle'. He used to visit our home, during festivals & various other occasions (like birthday etc.). Along with my parents & other relatives, he used to advise us, how much to save for future education, marriage & un-foreseen emergency situations.

He use to give personalized advise related to 'in which bank scheme', we should deposit money, which type of loans we should take for house building or repair. In a nutshell, he used to help us in our money management & achieving financial freedom.

Once I moved to a big city for job, I really felt lost. Big cities have many banks & many facilities... but no-one to advise me, based on my needs.

Instead of being just the provider of some specialized services, banks can offer holistic financial freedom solutions. They can provide intuitive solutions to all kinds of financial aspirations of customers.

The 'WHY' of banks should be "Money Management & Financial Freedom' for their customers, based on each customer's individual need & aspirations. Just don't segregate your customers (and put them into Gold/Silver/Platinum segments only). Move away from 'One Size Fits All' mentality.

Now you can interact/understand & serve each customer (not just a customer segment).

Banks should provide personalized banking service to all.

The Nike Case: Expansion Beyond Its Confines

Nike, originally touted to be a shoe company and having the logo- Just Do It, has of late transformed its initiatives via digital ways.

For Nike, the 'WHY' is, health of customer. To keep customer fit and healthy, they have rolled out many things, including various smart shoes.

The brand introduced the Nike App, Nike Training Club App, Nike Running Club App on social media channels. Also it offers podcasts on training, streaming of live workout sessions by experts, etc. So, we can see here that Nike has not limited its niche to just shoes but went out of the box to offer health solutions to its customers, influencing them to stay fit.

By figuring out its Why, Nike has not only stayed afloat in the market but also on the lines of disrupting its own business model and shifted to new business planes.

The Netflix Case: Exceeding Its Benchmarks

Netflix disrupted its own business model twice by simply figuring out its Why. In my opinion, NETFLIX wants to provide wholesome family entertainment, literally in the hands of customer. Movie streaming, TV soaps, Netflix Original on various smart devices (smartphone, tablets…) are just the way to achieve that "WHY".

Their constant brainstorming on their present model led them to find better solutions for entertainment. From renting out DVDs to streaming live movies to making its own movies, Netflix has come a long way to become a holistic entertainment solution provider to the viewers. It has figured out its Why and worked on the How to constantly lead the business in the entertainment segment.

Oil & Gas Industries

In my opinion, these companies should think of themselves as energy companies. Today, they are supplying Oil & Gas. But they should look at solar power or green fuel else they are likely to get wiped out.

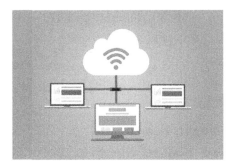

2. Integration with External Ecosystem

Remember, your customer is looking for a holistic solution. Your product, on it's own, may be solving one of his problem.

If your team & your product can collaborate with 'Partner+External vendors', seamlessly, you will be able to offer incredible solutions to your customers.

Of-course, your organization should have it's own quality standards for the criteria of integrations.

But organizations that have been successful in this pursuit understood this well in advance.

API (Application Programming Interface) & well-defined Micro-services are key for integration with external world. These will help you in making your system extensible as well as harness the power of 'Partner + External Vendor' eco-system.

FAAAN companies as well as many other companies like Mercedes-Benz Cars and Daimler Trucks have understood this power of collaboration.

You can visit https://developer.mercedes-benz.com to understand, how seriously Mercedes has taken API & Micro-service concept to roll out smarter cars for us.

Their website says:

"Welcome to Mercedes-Benz/developers! We support developers, Start-ups and enterprises in creating innovative applications with official vehicle-related data products, APIs and SDKs from Mercedes-Benz. Skyrocket your business models, join us in driving digital progress around mobility and beyond."

So here again, Mercedes had made sure that various external developer can create 'new applications' by using it's official vehicle related data.

API & Micro-Services (MS), which can integrate with internal & external system, can help you in bringing real transformation.

The readiness of interfacing with other products is key here & it all depends on the openness (or extensibility) of the underlying system.

API & MS can provide a holistic solution for a complete digital transformation, but your underlying system should be flexible enough so that it can be extended. Your partner or external vendors should be able to create new application, on top of your system.

If your underlying system is not open enough or if it can't be extended, all the efforts to go digital can fall flat.

Also, your management and staff should be open and adaptive for collaboration with partners. If your team is not ready to discuss/collaborate with external vendors, you will not be able to offer a fabulous & holistic solution to your customer.

In all these cases, to ensure that your system can be well-integrated with the external ecosystem, you can ask the partners to build, new solutions, on top of your systems. During this time, allow them to talk/interact with your team members.

Later, ask your team members to identify two good points and two 'not-so-good' points about partners.

Also, talk with partners & ask about their experience.

This exercise of creation of new solutions on top of your system as well as answers from your team members (about partners), will tell you a lot about your system as well as about your team members.

Let us go through example of some companies, which had harnessed the power of collaboration.

Apple Phone

Most of us know that Apple is the key competitor of Samsung. What we do not know is Apple is also a major customer of Samsung's chips.

In another case, Apple has its own applications and it has also collaborated with other app providers. For example, Apple has two map applications- Google Maps and Apple Maps.

"App Store" on Apple phone contains, various APPs. These APPs are developed by persons, who are not part of APPLE company. APPLE has provided the platform & has made sure that external developers are able to put their APPs on this. By collaborating with external developers & partners, APPLE has made sure that it's APP store is one the best.

Same approach has been taken by other Android phone makers. Their "APP Store" also contains various APPs, developed by external developers/vendors.

Netflix

The biggest platform for streaming shows and movies on web, tablets or mobile devices from anywhere, anytime is the perfect example of integration with the external ecosystem.

Amazon Web Service hosts majority of Netflix application.

Netflix architecture is build using well defined Microservices.

It uses more than 600 microservices to develop and deploy its content services. For 24/7 uninterrupted services, scaling and efficient speed, these micro-services provide holistic user solutions.

Subway

To understand the concept & importance of micro-services, let me give one example from the non-technical field. Though, sub-way doesn't use micro-services, but they use the underlying concept.

Subway is one of the world's largest fast- food chains with more than 41,000 outlets across the world. Consider the ingredients like vegetables, bread and sauces in the sandwiches as the microservices.

With these three types of ingredients, we can make 27 varieties of customized sandwiches!

Now suppose in a new country, subway wants to offer, different type of sandwiches by partnering with a local vendor.

That partner is good in supplying three types of local fruits. With this addition, subway can make 81 kinds of sandwiches. With the addition of new ingredients, the number of combinations increases and, hence, the food options for customers.

If Subway would pack all these sandwiches beforehand and sell them, then the option of customization and personalization would die, and the customers' choices could get limited here. Instead, Subway provides the option of instant packages prepared in no time using these different ingredients.

3. Breaking the Silos in an Organization

Robust Operational Platform

To bring about a transformation across the length and breadth of the organization, we must have a robust operational platform so that the new technology remains in sync with the operations of an organization, at all levels.

Around 1960, many companies started automation of their work by using technologies, available at that point of time. Now they have built & running with their own legacy systems (built 30-40 years back). They have grown so old over the time that it is difficult to bring a change in their systems. Their systems are often overlapping in terms of their functions, departments and processes.

During year 2000, most of the companies created cool websites and launched mobile apps. They declared themselves as 'Digital' companies, but behind them, there's most likely an old, legacy system running on old technology...a totally fragmented platform, somehow still working.

Let's have a look at some such cases.

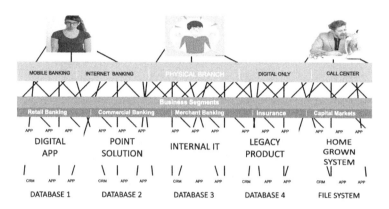

The Banking Case

Be it a big or small bank, the system silos remains difficult to break. There may be a bank having different branches/departments for different functions. Your bank may be offering you Loans, Deposit, Wealth Management, Credit Card…Insurance, Trade-Finance…

Though all these services are offered by a bank (under one name) but their individual systems have no interaction amongst themselves in reality.

The bank and the customers are the same, but all the data might not be in the same place. This is called Data Silos issues.

Majority of the time, banks are not aware of their overall exposure and limits for a variety of reasons. They have galaxy of systems/departments in backend to complete 'one simple' transaction…

These departments may have their own fabulous website but that doesn't match with the overall vision of the organization.

They are different mini-units collaborated under one umbrella. Various units for each vertical are created under one organization. Individually, all these units are well- automated & working.

But as many as 200 systems might be running in the backend & there is no sharing of data among them. In this case, the IT teams have to put tremendous efforts to connect the database and the respective systems. We may have moved on, but for these companies, backend system is still of 1980's era.

All these individual units are just aggregated under one CEO and given the face of an organization. It's quite a pity that many a times, CEO plays the role of aggregator here.

I am sharing my personal experience as a customer with a top Indian broking firm. The firm recently launched a good Stock Trading App. The mobile APP, on the face value, looked very smooth and frictionless. Within no time, they captured all my data, including KYC documents using the smartphone. The entire process took only 10-15 minutes. When I further enquired about the status of the final opening of my three-in-one trading account from the help desk, they told me that it would be done by the end of the day. I was surprised to know the reasons for this delay in such a prime broking firm. The reason was they had four systems (& hence four databases) located differently, and so the delay.

Only during 'End of Day' they run a cron/batch job, which collect & consolidate data for opening a new account.

As a customer, there was no instant gratification for me. Though the front-end looked cool, the overall customer on-boarding journey was pathetic. As an IT professional, I was hugely disappointed with such silos in their system.

Manufacturing Industries Case

A similar example can be observed in the manufacturing industries. You can find similar mini-units like the department handling the suppliers, the inventory management system, the logistic department, the accounts department, distributor, dealer-handling department, the sales team and the after-sales service department. If we look at the manufacturing industry as a whole, it's a single process. But the customer has to run from one department to another to procure the right information. The customer should either have enough time to move from one department to another or should have enough patience to hold on to the customer care calls, which ultimately drop due to the inefficient customer care professionals.

All these departments may be using:

1. Different development processes (Waterfall, Agile, Kanban, SaFE..)

2. Different technology standards, like REST, SOAP

3. Different UI technology stacks like Angular, React, Polymer

4. Different technology stack for backend systems.

5. It might also be possible that they might be using various point solutions, standalone product, or legacy solution for different departments/functions.

Just think of the plight of the IT head of this group. He must be putting a lot of effort just to make sure that, these internal systems (built with different technology stack & protocol), are able to talk with each other (that is, these internal system are able to share data with each other).

You have to ask yourself "Can you get full data for your customer in real-time basis, without any manual intervention?"

If the answer is NO than you are in trouble.

We must untangle this and move to a robust platform for the effective implementation of the right digital transformation.

Let us look at the next ground challenge.

4. Environment and Culture

Transformation-One Critical Missing Point

The change should always come with cultural transformation. Let me explain this further.

Tell me if $(A*B*C)$ can be lesser than $(A+B+C)$. Yes, it can be, if $C = 0$. Now, what happens if $C = $ CULTURE and you are attempting 'Transformation' by ignoring cultural transformation.

What are these cultural silos that make or break the digital transformation?

I have listed below some challenges, which are almost common across various organizations:

1. **Agility in Recruitment:** How long is the recruitment cycle - from written exam to final interview? Still 12 weeks? Why will any talent want to join your team if you are not providing instant gratification/results?

2. **Innovation:** If you are following Six Sigma, will you tolerate failures? Scale learning over scaling efficiency!

3. **Appraisal:** Reward outcome continuously. Don't wait for the annual appraisal cycle.

4. **Remove Layers:** If you still have four layers between your developer and customer, the chances are the developer is not working on real requirements.

5. **Labs:** Have a Sandbox where employees can experiment and learn. Use AR/VR to simulate. Leaders: Use social media; it's not a distraction. Are you using your own product? Whether, you & your team members use your product in real life? Or are you expecting customers only to use it? Eat your own dog's food.

One big challenge in the assimilation of this digital transformation across all the layers of an organization is its cultural makeup. From A-listed companies to start- ups, the cultural blockages have prevented the right digital transformation.

CoOpetitive is the new mantra. Rather than being competitive in today's business scenario, look closely at many big ventures where the two partners are not just each other's biggest competitors but also the collaborators in the same space.

Cooperative +Competitive = CoOpetitive

Many FAAAN companies use each other's services yet are each other's competitors.

In the case of Amazon and Netflix, both compete in the same space of a video streaming platform, but they are also collaborators. Netflix uses Amazon Web Service as the cloud platform to host, majority of application.

Apple and Samsung have been seen as the biggest competitors in the smartphone marketplace, but as I mentioned earlier, Apple is the biggest consumer of Samsung- manufactured chips for its phones. So, there is an evident change in the cultural behaviors of the product and service providers.

Cross-Pollination of Ideas

It has been seen in various organizations that there is a lot of departmentalization of seating arrangements. Different departments do not sit together in the organization. In such cases, we can least expect the interdepartmental mingling of the teams. This aspect is very important in bringing about a true digital transformation.

When the teams break the silos among them, it is easy for the employees to know each other, assimilate and appreciate each other's diversities. These diversities begin with cultural aspect of the company and extend to the technical know- how about each other's work. There is a huge scope for cross-pollination of ideas. This kind of smoothness in the relationship among the team members often manifests at the customer-level interaction.

The Communication Structure

Many of us have grown into the 'Control &Command' model. For the true experience of digital transformation, the hierarchy of communication should be such that it is transparent and open.

Let us take an example of a meeting where the managers are comfortable if the problem related to their group gets discussed in a common meeting without discussing first with them. I believe, this is a rare case.

We will find that too much of such hierarchy in the structure kills the team's ideation spirit. An open-door policy to management is essential in maintaining a transparent culture in any organization. The ideas of transformation should not see the hierarchy. It must reach the decision-makers fast for transformation.

The managers, the HRs and the staff - all must collaborate with the stakeholders for a holistic digital transformation program. They should plan the transformation strategy along with their internal staff, customers, partners and competitors.

The Mindset Gap

This challenge begins at the HR level. The recruitment criteria and internal promotions are still traditional. The vertical ways of working are such that we rarely empower our junior team members to take decisions.

There is a huge gap in the thoughts between a young intern and a higher management level professional in terms of adopting technology in their ways of working. On one hand, the young recruits are excited about the advent of new technology, while the top management is skeptical of the deliverance of the technology. One is super excited about testing it for better efficiency in their work, while the other one is reluctant to adopt it due to the comfort zone provided by the previous old-age technology. One can clearly see the difference in the basic mindset.

Encourage Failures

Many a times, we hear from senior leaders (especially during marketing calls) that they encourage failure. But the reality is quite different. Finally, everyone wants a salary and you would get it only when you are able to successfully ship something to your customer. Your customer will not pay you for a failed product/experimentation.

Failure is not allowed as we know that it is the outcome of experimentation and innovation. So, the culture of innovation and experimentation is not encouraged. Now, what is secret sauce here!!! In my opinion, the trick here is to allow small and fast failures.

We cannot expect people to succeed in the first attempt at a new technology trial. This does not mean that we are encouraging the culture of failure. There is a probability of both. By acknowledging failures, we are giving room to cultivate the culture of innovation.

To encourage failures, the corporates can introduce the 'Best Failure & Learning Award'. Here, it will be interesting to see how many members apply for these awards & are candid enough to discuss their failures in open.

'Fail Fast, Fail forward, Learn Fast & Scale Fast' is the need of the hour for better innovation.

Also, you can ask your junior team members, how many ideas they have got from non-reporting managers.

In majority of the cases, you will realize that 'team members' are getting advised/mentored/coached...and may be protected by their reporting managers only. Is this the correct method for grooming of your talents?

Netflix and Failure Handling

Netflix is one company that has allowed and integrated small and timely failures so that the platform knows well how to respond to the 11th-hour failure and how to stay equipped to handle it.

Netflix majorly focuses on regular quality checks to meet business needs. These automated quality check processes ensure consistency and efficiency in their operations.

Netflix focuses heavily on the quality attributes of it's application, which includes robustness as well as reliability.

Netflix believes that the only way to handle failure comfortably is to practice failing constantly. To achieve this kind of quality, Netflix engineers set about automating the failure.

To achieve this result, Netflix dramatically altered its engineering process by introducing a tool called Chaos Monkey. As the name suggests, the script lets the Netflix developers to be efficient enough to handle the chaos of automated failure.

As we know that there are innumerable components required for providing a reliable video stream to customers across a wide range of devices, it needs to be failure-resistant. Chaos Monkey is a script that runs continuously in all Netflix environments. It creates chaos by shutting down the server instances randomly. Thus, the Netflix developers are made accustomed to operating unreliable services and handling unexpected outages environment constantly. The developers have an opportunity to test the software in unexpected failure conditions.

Chaos is created while coding. Netflix incentivizes the developers to build fault-tolerant systems so that their day-to- day job is less frustrating handling the real-time failures. This way, Netflix designed their systems to be modular, testable and highly resilient against back-end service outages right from the start. So, Netflix makes its platform failure-resistant by altering the development process and using automation to set up a system, which is efficient enough in any condition.

We should not focus too much on preventing failures. Instead, we must build a culture of how to recover & learn from failure. If someone has failed, it should be seen as an attempt at solving a problem. In this evolving digital world, for innovation to succeed, be ready to fail, many times.

The subordinate staff should get the required support from seniors. Instead of not allowing room for failure, we must encourage the approach of Fail Fast, Learn Fast and Scale Fast.

Let us encourage smaller failures and learn the lessons from them. Such regular lessons pave the way to find solutions for the problems and, hence, scaling those solutions faster.

Earlier, the system & underlying processes were built to optimize efficiencies and minimize operational variance.

In manufacturing plants, a well defined assembly line was put.

Here, the goal was to achieve say only four defects per million of units produced.

To achieve this, companies were following either six sigma or CMMi. And yes, these were good processes, but may be 4 decades back.

But now, in knowledge industry, the case is different. We have to encourage new ideas and fresh thoughts, and for that, we can't set the goal of 'only four defects per…'. There will be failures. Encourage and learn from that. Handling failures must be a part of mastering success over a long period.

If Steve Jobs was worried about failures, we would have got phones with only better voice quality. By encouraging experimentations & failures, Apple launched Smartphones… and they keep on launching new/enhanced Iphones by doing continuous experimentations.

The Role of Recruitment Process in Digital Transformation

Human resources are the biggest assets of any organization. The right recruitments can make or break the future of the company. The organizational goals, its mission and vision, all are directly related to right hiring. The competencies should not just include technical aptitude but also the behavioral skills like problem solving, teamwork, innovative thinking and leadership. The HR team has a lot of responsibilities in this sense. They should have a knack of mapping a smart candidate. An organization must prepare a fertile ground for the overall growth of the recruits, which includes both professional and personal growth. Instead of focusing more on the past work, the hiring managers must have the foresight to see what potential the candidate has in terms of contributing to the long-term growth of the organization.

• **Checking Soft skills during recruitment**

You need to check this, during initial levels of the hiring process. During hiring, don't just look for hard skills. You have to come out with ideas to check soft skills.

Let me give one example here.

During recruitment process, give different kinds of exotic materials to the all the candidates, ask them to decorate a room, and look at the way in which the candidates work.

Remember, these candidates may not know each other, may never have decorated a room.

If they are able to work together, maybe they are good team player.

We might find some candidates to be very enthusiastic about decorating the room, while some might not be interested at all in such aesthetics; there might be some who will decorate it just for the sake of doing it.

Some candidates may take a leadership role here., while others will be happy just following the orders.

Some candidates may come up with 'out of box' ideas to decorate the room.

A lot can be deduced from this in terms of their behavioral indicators in the workplace.

• Attitudinal Competencies

During the recruitment process, we have to figure out the problem-solving skills in the potential recruits rather than selecting them on the same old traditional basis–looking at their merits and degrees. The criteria for selection have to be broadened. The aptitude and the attitude along with the EQ have to be measured as a part of the recruitment matrix.

• Treatment of Their Subordinates and Team Members

We must also look for other behavioral traits, like how the prospective recruit treats subordinates and other team members.

So during the recruitment process, monitor the behavior of candidates.

Watch, how they are behaving with office security guards, office boys or the person serving tea etc. This will tell you a lot about candidate's ethics and empathy skills, which is an important parameter of someone's EQ.

Piano Experiment

In the long run, money cannot be an eternal motivator in the career ladder. So, what motivates a candidate to perform on par in the workspace? To know this, we can do this experiment.

In one room, put a piano. Now Identify the brightest person from your team (who has never learned or played piano). Let's say the team member name is John.

Tell john that, he needs to in that room (with piano) for next 24 hours. Also, he can't contact outside world.

Now after 24 hours, if John can play piano, he will get 1Million USD.

Can he do that? I believe the answer is NO. So that tells that money alone can't be the motivator here.

Now in this case, observe how John approaches the problem of 'piano playing'. Whether John is even trying, or he has just given up (that he can't play piano).

HR can do similar experiment, while hiring candidates.

Here, the HR should look for the problem-solving skills of the candidate and how the candidate approaches the problem.

This can be a big indicator of a problem-solving mentality of a candidate.

In real life, there will be many situations, where your employee will be faced with an ambiguous situation or a situation, which had never happened before.

You need team members, who are ready to try new things & don't give up in crisis situations.

During COVID-19 pandemic times, I am sure, you must have discovered many gems among your team. Personally, I have seen, many of my team members, who volunteered & came up with out of the box solutions to handle this situation.

• Define the correct problem

In one such experiment in an art school, Sai (my friend) brought two tables. On one table, he put 40 objects, normal as well as exotic (used in school for drawing). He asked the students to select objects from the first table and create a drawing on the second table.

It was observed that some children examined a few objects, finalized their ideas quickly, and drew a design. The other set of children took more time, checked all objects, turned/rotated those objects, and took longer to complete the drawing.

This experiment concluded that group 1 was trying to solve a problem, where the major focus was on how they could produce a good drawing quickly.

In contrast, group 2 was trying to find a problem like 'what all types of good drawing can I produce?'

So which group will come up with new ideas in future? I believe, Group 2 will succeed as they are good at defining & refining the problem.

• The Pencil Experiment

In another such experiment, the candidates can be given a particular object like a pencil and may be asked to deduce the number of uses a pencil can have. Such experiments will help the hiring manager to know the candidate's different approaches of thinking and creatively solving a problem or viewing it as an opportunity or crisis.

These can be very clear indicators of the most required traits in innovation and experimentation of an organization as to where to look for the problem and how to solve the problems. A lot can be deduced about the EQ of a candidate here.

Let me give one more example from Taj Hotels.

Taj hotel Mumbai, India was attacked by terrorist on 26 NOV 2008. Not ONE Taj employee abandoned the hotel and ran away, but stayed right through the attack. They helped the guests escape and, in the process, many employees died. It confounded psychologists!

Finally, they pin pointed 3 recruitment strategies:

1. Taj did not recruit from big cities, they recruited from smaller cities where traditional culture still holds strong.

2. They did not recruit toppers, they spoke to school masters to find out who were most respectful of their parents, elders, teachers and others.

3. They taught their employees to be ambassadors of their guests and not ambassadors of the company.

Internet Source: The Ordinary Heroes of the Taj Hotel: Amazing Case Study - Study Mumbai

This example illustrates the importance of Soft skills & how to truly take care of their customer. Remember, in any company, it's the customer, who finally pays the salary of each employee (and not the finance or account department).

Many colleges do not teach soft-skills and emotional intelligence. Many 'brilliant computer graduates' can tell you how a computer works. But they will not be able to tell, how their own mind works. No one would have told them about 'self-awareness, empathy, compassion and creating something new'. They were always encouraged to compete against each other and get more marks than their friends.

So, they just don't know about 'teamwork'. They were encouraged to learn some subjects and answer the question 'correctly'. So how they will even know, what creativity means and importance of creating something new, something which no one has earlier thought of.

The Final Words

We need to understand these 'WISE' problems and 'really' solve this. I have seen, many organizations failing while attempting to do Digital Transformation. It may sound weird, but for Digital Transformation, you need to first take 'Inside Out' Approach. No technology can solve these WISE problems.

These are the debts accumulated over the years. Unless, you get rid of this, any approach/solution for Digital Transformation will be tactical at best.

CHAPTER 4

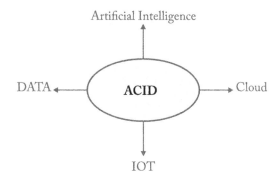

SOME STANDARD DEFINITIONS: ACID

Before we start getting to know about the four pillars of digital transformation, we must get familiar with the language used in these chapters involving the ACID formula.

ACID is the acronym for these four pillars of digital transformation:

- Artificial Intelligence
- Cloud
- Internet of Things
- Data

Glossary of Statistic Terms

Descriptive Statistic

It describes the primary feature of the data being studied. One example of this can be finding out the best-selling item in a furniture shop.

Inferential Statistics

This statistic is used to draw a conclusion that applies to data. An analysis is done on a subset of data. They give the probability.

Data Mining

It refers to the automation of exploratory statistical analysis on an extensive database to get patterns and insights.

Probabilistic Programming

It is the learning system that makes decisions in an ambiguous situation by taking inference from earlier experience or knowledge. It helps in the concept formulation.

System That Acts

It acts as per the defined rules, e.g., the fire alarm.

System That Predicts

It analyzes the data and arrives at probability decisions. Example: Based on shopping patterns, Target shopping mall, was able to identify pregnant women.

System That Learns

This kind of system arrives at probability and learns by abstracting, finding patterns, and identifying components.

System That Creates New Things

Here, systems are able to create new original stories, novels & songs.

Example: Shimon the singing songwriting robot has been taught to write his own lyrics by studying tens of thousands of songs written by the musical greats.

Developed by researchers from the Georgia Tech Center for Music Technology, the robot collaborates with human musicians and even has an album out in the spring.

The robot was given a dataset of 50,000 lyrics covering all genres including rock, hip-hop, jazz and progressive as part of its song writing education.

System That Relates

Applications like Siri or Alexa use EQ to do sentiment analysis from the text, voice or facial expression.

System That Masters

Humans are born with mastering skills. A new-born knows how to get milk; kids quickly learn how to identify a horse or a cow. We abstract the data, transfer and apply it to other places. For example: the human mind can easily differentiate between an Indian cow & Swiss cow.

System That Evolves

A system can dynamically change its design and adapt to the new environment. Our brain has evolved over the years by genetic mutations.

Supervised Learning

When we give training to computer-labeled training data having a paired input and output, it is called supervised learning.

Unsupervised Learning

It happens when unstructured data is given or does not have labeled paired data based on a similarity group or a pattern.

LinkedIn and Facebook use this to create a group for us by collecting data like–the place of graduation, geographical location, the company where we work, etc.

Semi-Supervised Learning

This is in-between learning. In the real-world, data is not clean. Here algorithm helps users to find out the correct output for new input. Netflix uses this semi-supervised learning for a recommendation system.

Reinforcement Learning

This is learning by trial and error. The computer knows through actions, feedbacks and algorithms.

Deep Learning

This kind of learning builds algorithms by using different layers of artificial neural networks like how our biological neurons are connected and work.

Note: These are standard definitions and taken from Wikipedia.

CHAPTER 5

THE FIRST PILLAR OF DIGITAL TRANSFORMATION: ARTIFICIAL INTELLIGENCE

Artificial Intelligence (AI) is one of the four digital transformation pillars, namely ACID(AI, Cloud, IoT and Data). AI has completely transformed the way we do business.

Artificial Intelligence, by definition, is the simulation of human intelligence by machines. Artificial Intelligence includes Machine Learning (and has the ability to learn and mimic human minds). Intelligent machines mimic the human mind traits, for example, problem-solving and learning behaviors. AI mimics our minds so well that sometimes its decision-making matches exactly what we might have thought. It can be both positive and negative development when we look at it from a long-term perspective. But, here first, we will discuss the positive aspects of intelligent machines.

AI has been the game-changer in terms of delightful customer experiences and processes. This technology has brought a new lease of life in creating and innovating ways of doing business. It has not only automated most of the human brainstorming process but has also led to massive revenue generation in certain sectors. The risk factors in business analysis have reduced significantly as most of the decision-making processes are now in the ambit of Artificial Intelligence.

As per a study by Forrester regarding Artificial Intelligence in the business prospects:

- 71% said AI has improved business efficiency
- 59% said it led to scalability
- 55% said AI helped in mapping consumer behavior in product development

Another research report says that 52 % of the customer switches to other brands if they do not get personalized services in a product.

In the age of instant gratification, where people hate to attend customer support calls, there must be a system available in the organizations that can direct them to the right service representative to solve their queries. To direct customers towards the right solution, the system must be brilliant to sense customer issues. This is prominent where Artificial Intelligence supports the service industry.

Banking and AI

Let us take the banking sector to explain the process further. Earlier, we would write an algorithm or computer rules to do regular banking work like interest calculation; this depends on whether the particular account was closed early or if the amount was varying or the interest rate had changed. There are many cases like this, where it is tough to encode all the rules or the algorithm.

Now Artificial Intelligence can take cognizance of all these factors based on the data's variation.

AI helps the computers learn without being explicitly programmed. It is able to do this because of various built-in features namely speech recognition, image classification, deep learning and reinforcement learning. It requires a robust training with variety of datasets & existing business scenarios.

Once all these are provided, AI can arrive at the initial algorithm to do 'Complex computational work' for present scenarios.

Now the beauty is that, after the initial algorithm, AI can keep on improving it's own algorithm based on different data sets & can start solving, new scenarios, on it's own (without any human intervention).

Looks too far fetched!!!....Keep on reading! With Reinforcement learning (which is part of AI), it's already happening

Artificial Intelligence can also, create better money management solutions in the future. It creates investment strategies that can lead to efficient money management. With the help of AI, we can invest on our own, based on our risk appetite & long term goals.

Earlier, one used to fill up boring forms to determine his/her risk profile. No more!!! Now, based on your earlier data (the habits of spending, saving, travelling & hobbies etc..) machine can tell & create a better risk profile for you.

So, banking has a significant scope of reinventing its business strategies using Artificial Intelligence and providing us with better financial solutions.

Teaching How to Fish

As the saying goes, you can give a person a fish to eat every-day or you can teach the person, how to fish. With AI, now we no longer are teaching the machine. Instead, machines are learning on their own, how to learn.

The resurgence of AI is majorly credited to the below two factors:

- The decreasing cost of cloud computing
- The availability of big data

There were two scenarios in case of executing the algorithm earlier.

In the first case, there were prediction models like the inventory forecast, market demand, etc., but those models worked with the sample data only. With the advent of AI, anyone can utilize the power of CLOUD computing and the BIG data to feed its prediction algorithm and get almost accurate results.

Secondly, as we know, computers, are traditionally good at executing a well-defined complex formula, such as computing Account Interest, as discussed in the banking example earlier.

The algorithms were developed to tell the computer how to recognize an object. For example, software code was written to identify how a DOG or a CAT looks like. So, in that process, one had to write complex codes to identify different types of CATS. As long as a correct algorithm is written, the computer will execute the program very fast for multiple sets of data. Still, on its own, it is not able to define or modify the algorithm.

As you must have guessed, it was becoming very difficult.

There was a lot of excitement in the initial days. But coding complex algorithms was becoming tougher & tougher. Expectations were high & results were not able to match.

After initial excitement, we saw '2 seasons of AI winter'. First season was around 1970. Second season was around 1995.Not much happened in the field of AI, during these times.

In my opinion, we have seen new excitement in this field, after Machine Learning (along with it's 3 major learning paradigms) came.

In Machine Learning, these 3 learning paradigms are there.

1. Un-supervised learning (UL)
2. Supervised Learning (SL)
3. Reinforcement Learning (RL)

Reinforcement learning is the most powerful concept.

Reinforcement learning is about taking suitable action to maximize reward in a particular situation. It is employed by various software and machines to find the best possible behavior or path it should take in a specific situation.

Reinforcement learning differs from the supervised learning in a way that in supervised learning the training data has the answer key with it so the model is trained with the correct answer itself whereas in reinforcement learning, there is no answer but the reinforcement agent decides what to do to perform the given task.

With Reinforcement learning, we can say that now AI has introduced the feature of "HOW TO LEARN" in the machine itself. That is with Reinforcement learning, machines are learning on their own and becoming smarter after each interaction/usage.

Some points related to Reinforcement Learning (RL):

1. RL can be used in robotics for industrial automation.

2. RL can be used to create training systems that provide custom instruction and materials according to the requirement of students.

Internet Source: Reinforcement learning-Geeks for Geeks

The bigger the data, the better the machine-learning and mapping of the human mind activities.

Earlier, whenever a small company tried to become big, scaling was a big problem. Many small companies are still struggling to become big (as becoming big means, you have to handle more data).

But now, it's the other way around. Machine-learning has altered this concept. Machines are learning with labelled input & output data.

With BIG data and the power of CLOUD computing, our computers are learning & improving, almost on an hourly basis.

Based on these results, the machines adjust their learning algorithms and keep improving them. The more the data input, the better the output.

We termed this to teach the machines how to fish with the help of Artificial Intelligence. Computers are now learning how to fish!

Artificial Intelligence-The Work of the Future

As per Daniel Kahneman's book 'Thinking, Fast and Slow,' we usually have two modes of thinking- Mode 1 and Mode 2.

Mode 1 is fast, automatic and takes less effort. It is more intuitive. On the other hand, Mode 2 is slow, conscious and analytical. It can do a lot of computations. In my opinion, the work related to Mode 2 can be done by machines, in the future. The work-related to Mode 1 must be assigned to humans only, *i.e.* the work that requires highly cognitive, social and emotional skills.

It can be the following skills:

1. Making the decisions in an ambiguous situation.
2. Teamwork where collaboration and understanding another person's perspective is important.

Machines can do the codified work. These machines can predict the future of the work based on past data.

But finally, machine work and human judgment is required in everything.

With respect to Artificial Intelligence, we can safely say: "Don't worry about your current work's future rather worry about work, which will be required in future."

When I talk about AI, everyone seems to ask one question—what humans will do, when everything get automated?

In my opinion, many processes or work will be automated, which, surprisingly, might include your current work as well!

Imagine a world with driverless cars and pilotless airplanes! With Artificial Intelligence, it seems to be possible in the near future, but does that generalize that AI will replace human Intelligence or jobs?

We have always been suspicious of the same whenever a new technology emerged. It also happened during the industrial revolution, but we devised new roles and responsibilities with the coming of the machines.

Again, with the advent of computers and the internet, globally, we feared that they would snatch our manual works. Still, we evolved to much better profiles, including processing these machines in many better-evolved roles. They never really put us out of work. These fears, I bet, haunt us due to over-watching Hollywood Sci-Fi movies.

Looking at the current scenario from a different perspective, I see that we will have to explore the type of work that only humans can do in the future.

I believe that the future will be about augmentation(by juxtaposition of humans and machines) and not just automation (by machine alone).

Now, how do automation and augmentation sort out the dilemma of AI replacing human roles? As a process, automation replaces human decisions and action by technology, with a combination of hardware and software. On the other hand, augmentation proposes that technology supports and improves human behavior in making decisions and taking actions. Machines can augment human skills and produce wonderful work if we align both of them in the right space.

Now that we have learnt about reinforcement learning, let us revisit the earlier banking example.

In a bank, let's say Peter wants to open a deposit account. So, these are the steps

1. Peter deposits the required amount say USD 1000.

2. The bank & Peter agree on the duration of the deposit account & the interest rate (say it is for one year with 8% interest rate). Also, they agree on the penalty amount, if deposit account is closed before 1 year.

3. Later, Peter, after 2 months, deposits some more amount say USD 250, in the same deposit account.

4. After 6 months, Peter withdraws, say USD 800 from this account.

5. Peter pre-closes this account after 10 months.

6. Also, there could have been some backdated or reversal transactions put on this account, due to variety of reasons.

7. So the bank has to calculate proper interest amount, taking into consideration that earlier Peter had added more (USD 250) into his deposit account but later pre-closed the account.

Now, the machine will surely require initial algorithm from a software developer to calculate Peter's deposit's account interest.

But after going through many similar cases like this, machine can keep on improving its algorithm and handle all cases related to 'Pre Closure of account, Change in Interest Rate/Maturity period of account' etc. No need for a new software code by a software developer. With reinforcement learning, machine can continuously, keep on enhancing itself to handle un-foreseen cases.

Also, if machine finds out that Peter always behaves like this (that he opens the account for one year but closes within 10 months), it can tell the human banker about this.

The banker can consult Peter & understand the reason behind this behavior. There can be some genuine reason behind this (say Peter has to pay his son's school fee after 10 months or …something like that).

In this case, the banker can suggest a better suited 'deposit product' to Peter. Win-win for all.

Courts, Judgements and Artificial Intelligence

Artificial Intelligence can serve and protect citizens by enabling effective and unbiased law enforcement. By scanning the massive database piled over the years in minutes, it can support the legal teams to make better decisions without any bias. The role of Artificial Intelligence in the legal system will be a big add-on in fast-tracking the judgments. Artificial Intelligence can aid the legal sector in providing efficient and better services in the following ways.

1. In a court case, machines will be able to advise whether or not a convicted person should be given parole, based on his record. The final decision can, then, be taken by

the Judge. The human elements involved in taking the right and a just decision can be easily left to the Judge.

2. If someone is filing a patent for new ideas, today, a lot of effort is spent identifying whether this idea is novel, and not duplicate. Machines can do that work efficiently. The final patent can be issued only after a human review. The intermediate process of scanning can easily be automated with the help of machines, thus, saving a lot of energy. AI can be used for regulatory and accessibility testing. Improved compliance can reduce potential legal costs.

Medicine and Artificial Intelligence

AI application can be extended to the medicine and health sector, saving a lot of energy by taking important decisions. AI application will identify and remove the fake positive cases.

It can quickly scan all the medical reports, go through the vital parameters related to human body & accurately detect, the root-cause of any illness.

Mental Health

Let us say you visit a psychiatrist for consultation. Based on the fed symptoms, Artificial Intelligence can very well prescribe the right medicine, but to identify those symptoms, one needs to talk to the patient. Only a great doctor will be able to ask the right questions, give the right advice, and map the diversions in the patient's normal behavior. He will understand the look on the face, eye movement, posture and ways of talking, which are the key to know the gravity of the situation with respect to the mental health of the patient. It will require gifted human perception and intelligence.

In hospitals, doctors who have critical thinking and decision-making abilities will be in demand. In the mental-health department, nurses who can console and help a mentally disturbed person, will be required. The staff should be able to give contextual and highly personalized advice to others.

We can help students or employees by listening to phone conversations and doing sentiment analysis. Of-course, one must first get consent and take care of their privacy issues.

But remember, with technology, we can gauge the mood of a student. A timely help can be provided to students or team members, if they are under lot of stress due to work/ragging/abusive senior manager.

Elderly Care

Along with IoT and Big Data, Artificial Intelligence can create safe environments for elderly care. There is software that can map various health indicators and support in regular body check-ups. There are many examples in the industry to prove it, but the fact remains that the demographic trend in the well- being and care industry is a welcome change as far as elder and child care is concerned.

Cinema and Artificial Intelligence

Artificial Intelligence has already put forward its footsteps in the movie industry and redefined the roles and responsibilities of cinematographers. The movie industry gives a good clue of how the future will shape up via the narratives already shown in the movies in this regard, be it Hollywood or Bollywood. Although we have animated movies based on cartoon characters; we still love movies where real human beings are involved.

Cinema has evolved much in adopting Artificial Intelligence technology. The entire cinematic experience has been transformed not just for the viewers but also for the producers, directors, screenwriters, cinematographers and the entire cinema teams. Talking about 3D movies in terms of AI would be an old talk. Cinema has welcomed AI with open arms. There is software that has made the cinema process different from the traditional experience.

Cinema uses AI today in the following roles:

- Marketing activities
- Calculating the box office revenues
- Determining the production costs
- 3D printing Technologies for sets design
- Finding audience demographics
- Designing the movie trailers
- Determining the opening weekend revenue at the box office
- Script analysis and mapping the audience locations based on the script

Netflix presents a better model of adapting Artificial Intelligence in its operations. The machine collects the viewers' data and understands what we humans love watching. Based on that data, they produced super-hit shows like 'House of Cards' and, thus, manage to win the audience's hearts and revenue.

AI and Recruitment

Let us see understand the impact of AI in HR. Tomorrow, if AI replaces the recruitment profile, it will be a refreshing change for the HR as they are often engaged in repetitive works like scanning the applications, scrolling through the job sites, sending emails, phone calls, scheduling interviews rather than taking the interviews and zeroing on the right candidates. Artificial Intelligence can automate half of this repetitive and monotonous work. The HR manager can better focus his/her energies on selecting suitable candidates.

Artificial Intelligence will make us more human at work. The routine and monotonous work have taken a toll on our humaneness. Software like CRM can take care of scanning the sales prospects, mailing and following up. The managers can focus on maintaining rapport with the clients and making better business relationships. The human element can be expanded in such roles with accurate database management with AI.

At work, technology has robbed us of our creativity and uniqueness and made us like robots. Artificial Intelligence, by taking over the monotonous and repetitive works, will allow us to take-up new challenging roles and tap the maximum potential as humans.

The AI-enabled robots can anytime take over menial and monotonous tasks. The professions that are occupational hazard-prone like mining can very well use Artificial Intelligence as a technology. Artificial Intelligence, along with IoT-led technology, can create wonders for such industries.

The Final Words

I want to conclude the chapter with an interesting excerpt from Forbes, which clarifies how Artificial Intelligence can give us the required impetuous to digital transformation if we adopt them in our day to day lives.

"Machines and algorithms in the workplace are expected to create 133 million new roles, but cause 75 million jobs to be displaced by 2022 according to a new report from the World Economic Forum (WEF) called "The Future of Jobs 2018".This means that artificial intelligence growth could create 58 million net new jobs in the next few years. With this net positive job growth, there is expected to be a major shift in quality, location and permanency for the new roles. And companies are expected to expand the use of contractors doing specialized work and utilize remote staffing."

All these facts and figures substantiate that it is a good idea to welcome AI in our lives for a true digital transformation and make our lives smooth and simple.

CHAPTER 6

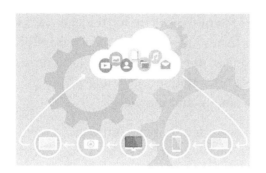

CLOUD: THE SECOND PILLAR OF DIGITAL TRANSFORMATION

Gartner predicts the worldwide public cloud service market will grow from \$182.4B in 2018 to \$331.2B in 2022, reaching a compound annual growth rate (CAGR) of 12.6%.

A true digital transformation has the main feature of 'ready-to-use' business solutions for both the consumers and the business owners. The solutions should be so simple that the stakeholders merely need to apply minimum efforts to make it a ready-to-use service. And CLOUD plays an important role to facilitate this.

In this chapter, let us brainstorm how the advent of CLOUD has changed the landscape of Digital Transformation and contributed to instant services.

Cloud refers to the on-demand computing services like computer networks, applications, processing and storage over the internet. It is a pay-as-you-go service for the end-users and the business providers. Instead of storing in huge hard disks or personal computers, we stash our data at a remote location at the servers owned by the big organizations accessible via the internet on computers, laptops and mobiles.

In simple words, big organizations like Amazon, Google and Microsoft have invested hugely in the servers to host our data; these are rentable as a service.

The major reasons for this transformation are cost-effectiveness, scalability and capacity flexibility in terms of usage.

Earlier, if you wished to start a new business, too many costs were involved, including the IT infrastructure - running a data centre, leased lines, the cost of physical hardware, the servers like CPUs, cores and RAM, storage, applications, constant monitoring of hardware to avoid any malware/virus etc. Cloud computing has waived off all these hassles and provided readymade solutions to set up an IT infrastructure.

History of Cloud

The use of the cloud metaphor for virtualized services dates at to General Magic in 1994, where it was used to describe the universe of "places" that mobile agents in the Telescript environment could go.

As described by Andy Hertzfeld:

"The beauty of Telescript," says Andy, "is that now, instead of just having a device to program, we now have the entire Cloud out there, where a single program can go and travel to many different sources of information and create a sort of a virtual service."

Internet Source: It 's The beauty of Telescript.docx- The beauty of Telescript says Andy|"is that now instead of just having a tool to program we have the complete Cloud | Course Hero

The use of the cloud metaphor is credited to General Magic communications employee David Hoffman, based on long-standing use in networking and telecom.

Apart from General Magic, this word/concept was also used in promoting AT&T's associated PersonaLink Services.

Around the 2000s, cloud computing became popular with the emergence of 'software as a service' such as Amazon Web Services.

In August 2006, Amazon created subsidiary Amazon Web Services and introduced its Elastic Compute Cloud.

In April 2008, Google released the beta version of Google App Engine.

In early 2008, NASA's Nebula, enhanced in the RESERVOIR European Commission-funded project, became the first open-source software for deploying private and hybrid clouds, and for the federation of clouds.

By mid-2008, Gartner saw an opportunity for cloud computing "to shape the relationship among consumers of IT services, those who use IT services and those who sell them" and observed that "organizations are switching from company-owned hardware and software assets to per-use service-based models" so that the "projected shift to computing... will result in dramatic growth in IT products in some areas and significant reductions in other areas.

Cloud provides the following services:

- IaaS -Infrastructure as a Service
- PaaS -Platform as a Service
- SaaS -Software as a service
- DaaS -Desktop as a Service

IaaS-Infrastructure as a Service

IaaS provides the IT infrastructure and resources to its subscribers. This infrastructure can be any IT service, operating systems, applications, middle ware, physical computing resources, security, backup, etc. IaaS manages our software's purchase, installation and configuration effectively over the internet. This infrastructure is provided to the subscribers in the form of a Virtualization feature, it is already discussed at length in previous chapters. A virtual machine monitor, as a host machine, called hypervisor runs another virtual machine called a guest machine for backup, security, data partitioning and scaling. Some of the examples of IaaS are Amazon Web Services (AWS), Cisco Metapod, Microsoft Azure, and Google Compute Engine (GCE).

PaaS-Platform as a Service

PaaS is a cloud-based model that provides an integrated platform for business applications. It gives a 360-degree solution to develop, run and manage business applications without building and maintaining the infrastructure required for the entire software development process. PaaS gives us holistic application solutions by building, testing, deploying, managing and updating the apps. It provides all the required tools - database management, Business Intelligence services - to set up a business app.

Few examples of PaaS are AWS Elastic Beanstalk, Windows Azure, Heroku, Google App Engine and Apache Stratos.

SaaS-Software as a service

In the SaaS model, the subscribers can rent the business software as on-demand software. It is a centrally-hosted service involving the development and support of the software as a paid service through the internet. Third-party vendor, as usual, maintains SaaS.

A few examples of SaaS are office software, accounting software, payroll software, ERP software, MIS software and CRM software.

DaaS-Desktop as a Service

DaaS was first introduced in the early 2000s as a subscription and cloud-based virtualization service. In DaaS, the third party manages the entire virtual desktop infrastructure - data storage, computing, networking, backup, security and up-gradation. The end users can access these back-end operations through client software or a web browser. These virtual desktops are hosted on cloud infrastructure, and the organizations can focus on managing the apps, security or images. It reduces the client's software license cost, which is cloud-hosted and internet-accessible.

Applications of Cloud

The applications of the Cloud are now seen in most of the fields right from our day-to-day banking operations to space explorations. There are evident reasons for Cloud's popularity at these organizations. Cloud computing has disrupted traditional business models. People, who are serious in their mission of being on the path of digital transformation, have already been the early adopters of the technology and are paving the way for other business models to increase the scope of this transformation.

Be it the cost-effectiveness or the elasticity quotient of the operations, the Cloud has provided a sustainable business solution that is ready to get started. Due to these advantages, many organizations have adopted cloud solutions and shown scalability in their operations; they are focusing on the core business functions and outsourcing the rest of the back-end IT operations to third-party vendors. Although there are several applications of cloud computing, we will focus on the IT and banking space in this chapter. The rest of the businesses have similar models to achieve true digital transformation based on cloud computing solutions.

Software Applications

Infrastructure Elasticity and Hardware Optimization

In banks, there was a time when bank used to put our software applications in large physical hardware boxes. The box sizes were based on peak volumes of the transaction for the software application. On normal days of operations, those boxes would remain partially utilized or idle. Only during month-end or year-end, when banks were supposed to do interest calculation for all accounts, they needed to start a parallel process to give a faster response.

To run a parallel process, banks require a good number of boxes. So, bank would buy and keep many hardware boxes for those 'Peak Days'. With the advent of CLOUD computing, now bank have the option to provision the required space just for peak days.

Watch for these four conditions for the usage of cloud technology to give the Digital Transformation in a real sense:

(a) When software application remains non-elastic, then there is no advantage of CLOUD.

(b) We have to figure out whether the application is elastic or not. On those peak transaction days, month-end or year-end, will the application bring up an independent new process? If it is dependent on some software, which isn't scalable, we will not be able to bring up a new process.

(c) If the application is NOT elastic, we will not get the benefit of the CLOUD.

(d) With CLOUD, you can bring up various services. This can help you if some services go down. So CLOUD (and lot of services), can help you in handling failure cases. If one service has gone down, work can be shifted to other services. So, your application can be running/working 99.99999 percentage of time.

To explain this further, let's take a hypothetical example. Suppose your company has only ten defined users, who always do "100,000" transactions daily. But there is no change in transaction load, throughout the year. That is to say that throughout the year, only 10 users will work & daily 100,000 will happen.

Also, you are not much worried about system, up & running all the time. Here, we would not have any advantage of CLOUD.

So, you should use CLOUD:

1. If you want to convert your Capex cost into Opex Cost

2. Transaction Volume on your system, varies on different days

3. You want your system to be up & running, 100% of time.

Banking System

Outsource H/W Maintenance

The cloud model has made banking operations more consumer-friendly and digitalized as compared to the traditional system.

Earlier, in the banking system, the IT team was responsible for the procurement of the right amount of hardware and the operating system in addition to its timely maintenance.

Now, banks can get all these as a service from a third party who is an expert in the maintenance of the software operations by the previously discussed IaaS, PaaS, and SaaS. The storage, backup and data security, everything is handled through third-party cloud computing outsourcing.

But be very clear on ' What Pay per Use' means. If bank has taken services of a banking software product, whether "Pay per use', mean that whenever bank person, uses an "Account Inquiry option", bank has to pay or when bank person 'Opens an saving account" than bank has to pay. What is the clear definition of 'Per use', when you are using any software application. Put special attention to this "Per Use' term and agree with your software vendor on this. Remember, that 'Account Inquiry' can be a very light transaction but 'Account Opening' is a heavy operations (in terms of data etc). Will you pay same amount for both type of usage.

Pay As You Use

These days, the banks can get extra hardware, immediately and with almost zero manual intervention; they just need to pay for what they have used.

Elasticity

As we know that the CLOUD is an 'On-demand Rental of Compute and Storage Hardware', it can sort out various banking problems like the year-end requirement of large hardware and small hardware or post-year-end operations. Earlier, they were forced to buy large hardware for their operations. Now, with the advent of cloud computing, banks can handle the 'Elastic Volume'. During the year-end hustle and operations, they can take big hardware on rent, to the tune of almost infinite for infinite computations. After the processing is done, they can release back this hardware.

Flexibility

With CLOUD, the major benefit, various industries have received over time, is that it can now focus specifically on their core business. The banks' IT team can concentrate their energies in providing a good technical solution for bank business problems.

Cloud computing manages CAPEX and OPEX budgets by providing cost-effective cloud solutions. It can shift the spending from capital expenditure (CapEx) to operating expenditure

(OpEx) in an organization as the companies will buy computing as a service rather than physical servers. This will decrease IT expenses on new projects.

Cloud and Space Exploration

The realizations of our dreams and ambitions are on the verge of touching the land of planet Mars. Space-borne data from satellites are useful for commercial and societal purposes. Cloud computing services can collect, evaluate, understand big data for real-time analysis and manage the gigantic amount of data.

NASA and Cloud

In the recently launched Perseverance Mars Rover, NASA has affirmed that cloud computing is an essential technology to process data in real-time through video footage and satellite imagery. It integrates all the terrestrial and space components data needed to provide the right analytics. NASA's on-boarding of the SG-100 Cloud Computing Payload, a radiation-tolerant processor is capable of processing data 12 times faster than any available counterpart.

AWS, Cloud and Space Exploration

In the coming years, we are set to see the launch of many satellites in the Earth's orbit with organizations like SpaceX building new constellations. Big satellite owners build and operate their own ground stations. The smaller companies, due to unaffordability, can't enter this satellite business as it requires a huge sum of money. But the good news is – the small satellite owners can own and run such stations with the help of third parties. As per the news, Amazon Web Services (AWS) has announced its cloud services to the satellite operators as well. The satellite owners can rent the AWS cloud services to send and receive data from orbit by Amazon-managed ground stations. This service will allow the satellite operators to get access on a pay-as-you-go basis and pay less for down-link time.

The Future of Cloud Computing

Despite its long history, cloud computing is still in an early adoption stage. Less than 30% of the workload is estimated to be transferred across the Cloud. Many organizations are still in the think-through stage of adopting it.

For a true digital transformation, organizations have to rethink their business processes & move to CLOUD, ASAP.

CHAPTER 7

INTERNET OF THINGS: THE THIRD PILLAR OF DIGITAL TRANSFORMATION

The Internet of Things (IoT) has brought a paradigm shift in technology and taken the world by storm by combining the real and virtual worlds. IoT has transformed our lives by connecting us in unimaginable ways. This technology is the key to digital transformation. It is invading everything around us and seeping into our daily lives too. This invasion has made things more comfortable and easier than ever before.

As per the definition, IoT (Internet of Things) is an ecosystem of interconnected sensors and devices collecting and exchanging data for intelligent intercommunication. It is one of the major players in bringing out digital transformation in our everyday lives; it has made our lives 'smart' by introducing those little devices around us; soon, I think, these devices will be a part of our day-to-day lives. This ground-breaking technology has a major role in bringing a remote culture of working and thinking, together.

We can measure the impact of IoT as to how big the arrival is. As per a research, it is expected that we will have a staggering 100 billion connected IoT devices and a global economic impact of more than $11 trillion by 2025.

As far as the medical sector is concerned, the progress is huge, and it is estimated to be a $543 billion industry by 2025.

The Internet of Things is now not just a technical topic but a part of our lifestyle, including social and economic aspects. After linking different devices, IoT has connected the threads of our lifestyles with each other.

We have entered an age where our communication mode is translating to the devices around us. Further, they are also exchanging, consuming and computing huge amounts of data every moment for better decision-making without any human intervention. We are now living in a hyper-connected world where all our activities have become a source of database and analysis for better decision-making technologies.

The Internet Architecture Board includes four common communication models based on how IoT devices connect and add value to our lives.

- Device-to-Device
- Device-to-Cloud
- Device-to-Gateways
- Back-End Data-Sharing

These devices collect the data and start the process of sensing, analyzing and acting on it. It brings the power of the Internet, Data Processing and Analytics for global interaction under one platform. This intelligent connectivity among the devices is making way for energy-efficient systems, which can be the foundation of the social and economic goals of any nation. These interconnected systems have already given us some of the smartest systems in the field of Energy Generation, Agriculture, Healthcare, Hospitality, Home Automation, Environment Management, BFSI, Retail, Warehousing and Surveillance.

We all must have heard of Google Maps using an Android phone's density on a particular road to tell whether there is any traffic jam.

Google tries to find out how many Android phones are there on a particular road. According to me, this was one of the first examples of Google using the IOT (by Android smartphones) concept to help us in knowing the traffic status.

Alexa and IoT

Alexa, a virtual assistant AI technology, has been one of the smartest home automation devices in the recent past. It is designed on the lines of APPLE's Siri and Google Now feature. Alexa Voice Service (AVS) developed by Amazon can voice-enable any connected device that has a microphone and speaker by intuitive voice commands to perform specific tasks.

Alexa can transform the entire landscape of energy sector.

For instance, it can monitor the electricity consumption in the house and connect them to cloud-based smart systems. This can compute and tell us how to save energy.

Welcome to a smart, automated home where we can connect the smart systems to Alexa, be it a door, glass break or a smoke sensor; this creates the picture of a perfect energy- conserved smart home.

These devices sense the human presence in an area and check the regulation of the energy requirements. With all the interconnected data and devices over the cloud, IoT devices can optimize Light, Heat and Temperature, Smoke, Fire, Water leakage, etc. These IoT sensors collect data, analyze the consumption and translate the analyzed data into information. The entire cloud-based system then reports this information to the users to help them make informed decisions; the process improves our homes' energy efficiency. This way, IoT creates an efficient and sustainable ecosystem of energy in a house.

Healthcare and IoT

IoT is now a significant part of the healthcare industry where technology allows medical professionals to connect with patients in a proactive way.

This technology has enabled remote monitoring and connected both the medicare professional and the patients in a better way.

It has increased the possibilities of healthcare and extended the boundaries of the medical world. Due to IoT, medical consultation and other healthcare services are now available even in the remotest corner of the world.

Right from doctor's consultation to critical surgeries, we have seen technology shaping the medical world for a better future. Let us have a glimpse at how IoT is redefining the medical sector and assisting the stakeholders better. Along with patients, hospitals, families, paramedical staff, insurance companies, all are the beneficiaries.

How does it work?

As per its architecture, the health sector uses ingestible sensors, monitors, actuators, contact lenses, detectors, camera systems inter-communications. These devices collect patients' data, aggregate, process digitally and upload it to the cloud. The advanced analytics infers the insights for better decision-making for medical professionals.

Looking at the current scenario, we can very well say that IoT has contributed positively. It can help even the senior citizens in maintaining their health. Devices like IoT-based blood pressure trackers, diabetes meters, asthma inhalers, glucose monitoring devices, cardiac rhythm monitors etc., keep a track of the health parameters of the elderly people and update the near and dear ones about their health conditions. If elderly people are staying far from their families, then IoT can facilitate their medical care. The devices collect important health data and send it across to the physician and the relatives. These actions facilitate better decision-making and health can be better-taken care of in case of remote conditions.

Apart from senior care, IoT also assists the younger crowd to track their health by keeping a check on their calorie count, exercise routine, doctor appointments, blood pressure and diabetes. The best part is that wearable fitness trackers are available to keep us well-informed about our health. If any abnormalities are noticed, then we can immediately connect to a physician for consultation and treatment.

These devices transmit the required data even when the patient is on the move; this is done via cellular mode by using a 'plug-and-play' device. The patient just needs to login, enter the password, and monitor the health parameters. These wearable biosensors, the X-ray machines, are connected to our Bluetooth or Wi-Fi network to streamline the entire healthcare data for better actionable insights.

Corona Vaccine and IoT

Considering the way things are going these days, we can expect IoT to assist the medics in the corona vaccine trials in the advanced phase. The IoT devices have already assisted us in monitoring our temperatures during day-to-day operations by being physically in touch with the doctors. This has also helped in maintaining a social distance between both the parties, thus, keeping the risk of infection at bay. The built-in sensors, smart algorithms and the advent of IoT have given appreciable support in fighting the pandemic.

In future trials as well, we can expect IoT to assist researchers in decoding the patterns of the spread of the disease in high-risk areas. The high-resolution computer-generated simulation and genome sequencing methods will be a big support to researchers. The IoT devices can compensate very well in case of a shortage of medical professionals. The arrival of bot-assisted treatment also called Co-bots can change the entire scene of treatment without risking the lives of medical professionals.

During the research, IoT can save a lot of time and effort by computer-generated simulation of the gene pool and fasten the drug trial process. The drugs, as we know, have to go through various phases, and the simulation is a part of it. IoT devices can check their effectiveness and efficacy. If researchers can decode all the genes of a human and grow them quickly, then elapse time can be reduced in the vaccine trial.

Digital Twin

One of the major features of IoT is DIGITAL TWIN. We have already heard about them, but let us have a look at the definition and how Digital Twins help the human race.

"Digital twins are software representations of assets and processes that are used to understand, predict and optimize performance to achieve improved business outcomes."

We can create a digital representation of any physical object. It helps heavy industries that use heavy physical objects - turbines, windmills and aircraft.

Let's discuss more with examples:

1. **Windmill:** We can create a digital twin of windmills running in a remote rural area. We can also put sensors on each windmill so that we get real-time data of each and every movement.

   Now, we can have a digital twin of each windmill in our urban office. Along with sensor data based on the weather forecast, we can predict which windmill will work properly or which may fail.

2. **Air-Craft Engine:** We can have a digital twin of the plane engine in our office. We can get the data related to the

plane journey through sensors. When the plane lands at a destination, we would know whether the engine needs any maintenance. So, with a digital twin, the time and cost can be lowered down.

3. **Medical-Gene Pool Analysis:** In drug trials, Digital Twins can expedite the process by testing the gene pool with AI and digital twin. Can this help us in the current situation? In case we have a full genome analysis of various healthy and sick people, we can use the digital twin concept to simulate and fast forward to bring out an effective vaccine.

IoT and Energy Sector

The application of IoT has extended to the energy generation sector as well. Electricity is now being generated safely and more efficiently with IoT. Smart Grids have been introduced to generate electricity.

Electricity, we know, is the foundation of any country's development. Generating this power has been directed towards IoT-ready solutions. IoT application has a lot to contribute in producing, saving and conserving this precious source of energy. Smart IoT-based electricity meters have been installed in many metropolitan cities of our country. The residential sector accounts for 60% of the electricity consumption in the power industry.

Many state governments have adopted the IoT-based approach to induce smart grids and meters to conserve electricity at the domestic level. TPDDL (Tata Power Delhi Distribution), which caters to the power needs of 7 million people in the Capital, has IoT-based smart meters. They integrate all the appliances of the home and report the energy consumption demands to its users to facilitate an actionable decision for conservation. Modular intelligent switches with radio frequency communication technology, integrated with smart sensors, control the appliances as per the need.

As per a World Bank Survey, by 2021, residential consumption would surge 260%. As a country with a 1.37 billion population, if we start focusing on conserving these precious resources through technologies like IoT, then we can progress faster on the way to the development curve.

Major oilfields across the world have been connected to market-ready IoT solutions. This Energy Management System developed with IoT can be the future blueprint of our sustainability efforts towards energy generation. We can say here the entire distribution, generation, management and consumption have been directed to IoT mode of operation.

Smart Cities

Under the Smart Cities Mission 2015, the Government of India decided to develop 100 smart cities based on the concept of IoT. These 'Smart' cities will have the core idea of sustainability in terms of resource conservation with an IoT-ready solution, starting from the homes to the streets to the entire smartly-planned tech cities. IoT will work as the heartbeats of these cities.

Home Automation and IoT

As per a survey report, the home automation market in India is expected to touch Rs. 30,000 crores by 2022. This market has a huge potential in terms of IoT-based applications. If you have bought a new home and invested the major earnings of your life in it, then you need to ensure that it is safe for your full family (for your elderly parents & kids). If you are a working couple, then the responsibility of safety increases all the more.

IoT-based door sensors, glass break sensors and smoke sensors can give us a perfectly safe and secure, energy-conserved home to take care of our near and dear ones. Any unauthorized person would think twice before breaking into your abode. The smart house cameras not only record the footage of intrusion with IoT applications but also send it to us in real-time to take a preventive step.

Danger of Pilferage

The fear of pilferage and door-breaking ends with smart IoT surveillance cameras. This gives us a perfect sense of security. Whenever somebody tries to break the glass and the sound above the threshold level gets breached, these cameras activate the inbuilt microphones, which are analyzed by the detector circuitry. The owners get alerted on the door breaking and can inform the police immediately.

Fire Breakage

There is a huge danger of dying of smoke in case of fire accidents at home. We must ensure fire safety in this case. IoT has made an intelligent intervention in this category too. The IoT-based smoke sensors can detect any kind of mishaps caused due to the break of sudden fire at home. The central alarm system fitted in the sensor detects any kind of smoke. The IoT technology can reduce such threats by up to 1/4th by securing our home from any such untoward incidents.

Energy Conservation

Imagine sleeping while watching TV and not switching it off and then waking up in the morning to switch-off appliances, including the TV! Imagine walking in the corridor of your home, and all the lights turn on and off sequentially as you march ahead in the corridor. Lights get switched off automatically in a room where no one is present and turns on as you enter! Doesn't that sound magical?

No. It is not magical. The Internet of Things has made it possible to conserve the maximum possible energy in our IoT-based automated home.

We can safely say here that IoT can provide a safe, secure, automated home that provides 24/7 live monitoring along with energy-efficient systems. This is called a smart home in real sense! The synchronization and integration of IoT technology in our residential space are now seamless and user-friendly, which makes our overall surveillance a smooth experience.

So, wake up to technology and keep the perimeter of that dream home safe with smart surveillance systems and Smart Technology!

Heavy Industries and IoT

The responsibility for worker's safety remains prominent when it comes to the mining sector; it happens to be one of the most occupational hazardous industries. Safe production in coal mines can be further promoted with IoT applications. The coal and mining industries deal with huge occupational hazards in terms of employees' health. IoT can be a big help here. There have been serious safety issues involved in the production and generation of the coal and mining sector. With the advent of IoT-based supervision, many serious accidents have been prevented till now. Attempts have been made to develop a multi mode sensing platform to implement IoT-based applications in underground coal mines, thus, ensuring a safer environment.

With IoT, we can do machine maintenance JIT (Just in Time). Earlier, one had to send machines or cars for periodic maintenance. In many cases, maintenance was done, even though it was not due and even if the machine parts were still in proper working conditions. In other cases, maintenance was done after a breakdown was reported. Now with IoT, we get real time data for each machine and its parts. It gives us room to make a judicious call on whether maintenance is needed or not.

On similar lines, if we can apply the concept of IoT to bridges or trains, we will come to know beforehand if something is wrong. Proactive action can be taken to stop the traffic movement on the bridge. All these can avoid accidents due to nearly crumbling bridges or public vehicles.

BFSI and IoT

As per a survey, the banking sector lost a total of Rs. 168.74 crores to organized crime directed at ATMs in the past three years. The recent changes in the BFSI (banking, financial services and insurance) sector like the internet, mobile and ATM banking have introduced such security challenges in terms of surveillance-related issues. IoT has come to the rescue of the entire BFSI sector. It has introduced some smart IoT-based surveillance. This kind of IoT-based video surveillance is accurate and reduces the number of false alarms. When they sense real-time human detection, they send an instant alarm in case of a perimeter breach. Visual verification has assisted in the insurance field, which has the backup of the exact incident for the coverage of the claims. These clippings are real-time and accurate, increasing the latitude of a banking surveillance system. Smart analytics triggers high-quality video feeds with video gateways accessible on any kind of video platform useful in BFSI surveillance.

The entire Banking, Finance and Insurance Industry is now connected on phones, laptops, storage devices and smart tabs to ensure peace of mind to all the stakeholders including customers and bankers alike.

If we look at the traditional surveillance systems, which had multiple cameras at every nook and corner of the bank or insurance premise, they have not been able to provide 360 degrees intrusion-free surveillance.

Installing multiple cameras with the web of wires to cover a wide area is now history, the new IP-based BFSI surveillance systems have replaced them all. Aesthetically, if we looked at the traditional security systems like CCTV cameras, they seemed messy. Just in case a single wire got disconnected somewhere, it could send chills across the security teams. The security purpose gets absolved then and there. IoT-based wireless BFSI surveillance provides relief from such a webbed security setup. They are easy to maintain and install and give a smart digital transformation to BFSI operations.

The ATMs and their branches can be monitored locally and remotely with a few smart cameras installed, without worrying about the wired set of multiple cameras getting disconnected, due to some untoward incidents like the ill intention of robbers or some natural hazards. These wide-angle cameras have better night vision; they cover blind spots and have higher resolutions. This way, there is superior outdoor and indoor perimeter surveillance installed.

As per a survey, the video surveillance market of India is expected to grow at a massive rate of CAGR of 22.96% from 2015 to 2022 to reach $8.24 billion. This is proof of the emergence of the IoT-based E-surveillance industry in the BFSI sector.

IoT and Retail

The retail sector has fast moved from the brick-and-mortar model to the e-commerce space, this has made it all the more tech-centric in its operations. Smart IoT sensors have mapped the customer behavior of the retail industry, and are now making marketing policies based on the collected data. They map the customer footfall and the activities a customer does in a particular shopping area. The devices capture their behavior. Everything is monitored in real-time with these IoT-based sensors, and the data is further sent to the centralized analytics department for detailed analysis. As per a study by Verizon, IoT has made an entry in the retail sector and has impacted the retailer's behavior in the following ways:

- Eighty-nine per cent of early-movers in retail gained insight into customer preferences and behaviors from the Internet of Things.

- Seventy-seven per cent of early movers in the Internet of Things in retail have created better opportunities in business collaboration and better customer experiences.

These smart sensors come with better surveillance and provide good aid to the Training and Development departments of the retail sector. They can map the employee behavior as per customers' interaction and train them as per their standards to provide the best services. There is better compliance adherence in the employees as there is a remote and centralized management monitoring all these employee parameters.

IoT and Warehouse Industry

Warehouses have, traditionally, been located on the outskirts due to space constraints. Therefore, monitoring these multiple warehouses and their operations has always been a challenge. The warehouse industry has witnessed huge losses due to multiple thefts. With the advent of IoT-based sensors, all the warehouses are now centrally connected and monitored in real-time in terms of operations and security.

IoT and Quick Service Restaurant Industry

Earlier, we had to go to restaurants to get our food packed and then we would bring it to our home, to enjoy with our family. Only some restaurants would take orders on phones and deliver them to our doorstep. Now, with the advent of ghost kitchens and quick service restaurants, the case is not so. The likes of Swiggy, Zomato and Food Panda are instant in their services to deliver us the best of the food items available, as per our choices and desires.

During this COVID time, many of us craved restaurant food, while at home. I am sure, many of us must have availed the services of Swiggy, Zomato or such food-delivery services to order our favorite food. So how do they do it?

The IoT technology has connected all these industries and made food services available at our doorstep. These cloud kitchens have the base of IoT sensors, and surveillance is not the biggest concern anymore. The light, heat, temperature and smoke sensors maintain the overall hygiene and the ambience of the restaurants and provide a delightful customer experience. IoT provides an ecosystem of unified hardware, software and cloud-based sensors to help these QSRs to capture real-time events, monitor and report their analytics for required action. The store opening, closing, its hygiene maintenance, cleanliness, buffet-readiness - all are maintained by cloud-based IoT sensors ready to give the best business experience. The operations now run more smoothly, which would have not been possible without this technology.

Final Words

This is the power of the new 'coming of age' technology - the Internet of (Every) Things, which has changed the entire landscape of many industries that are described above. This is just the beginning of it, and we are yet to see the best of technology.

For a true digital transformation, we need to have a system that can give us futuristic solutions, planning, monitoring and execution for the blueprint of the sustained models of business. IoT has given this kind of leverage to many industries and a lot more can be achieved with this in coming days.

CHAPTER 8

DATA-THE FOURTH PILLAR OF DIGITAL TRANSFORMATION

In the series of A.C.I.D, *i.e.* Artificial Intelligence, Cloud and IoT, we will discuss the last pillar of digital transformation– the Data.

Big Data today is fueling the Digital Transformation engine all across the globe. The organizations are on the path of chartering new business models; therefore, they combine big data- structured and unstructured - to enable digitalization and automation of their operations.

One of the top Indian industrialists once quoted that "Data is the new oil"; we will justify this further in the chapter.

Whatever transformations we have had previously, we have seen that though we produced new things, it was always difficult to scale. This is not the case with big data.

If this data is managed well, then it can transform the entire sales, manufacturing, inventory, logistic and after-sales service experience of an organization.

If we look closely, we all are the data sources for the forthcoming digital transformation. Even small details, like the choice of clothes on social media, become a data source for a cloth merchandising company.

When we scroll through Facebook and happen to come across a clothing brand whose one-piece is marked as 'Like' on their page. What happens next?

The next day, we see the same brand on our homepage timeline. We again click a like on their page.

The day after, we come across another similar clothing brand on the home page. Over time, we will notice that all of a sudden, we would start getting similar brand recommendations.

Ever thought about why and how these pages appear on our Facebook pages?

We fed the data of our choice on a social platform - here, Facebook -which has inbuilt AI in its system. This input data produced more similar output data, which might relate to our choices. This is just one example. We have been consciously and unconsciously feeding our data in the form of documents upload like identity cards, bank details, photographs, videos, shopping preferences, movie choices, destination preferences, skill details, resume on job-portal etc.

There are two types of Data:

- **Structured**
- **Unstructured**

Structured Data

Any data that can be easily searched in terms of the phone number, zip code, names, dates, addresses, credit card numbers, stock information, geolocation, etc. is structured. We can access this data from relational databases and spreadsheets across various places.

Unstructured Data

Any form of videos, photos, audios, presentations and web-pages, which are not there as per the pre-set data models is called unstructured data. This data is available much more than the structured data over various platforms and is the wealth of information that can be tapped via Artificial Intelligence technology to shape business ideas.

Tomorrow, you must not be surprised if someone hires a data analyst to carve out your profile by going through various social media accounts, namely, LinkedIn, Facebook, Twitter, or even credit card data. The machine, with the help of the entire database, can precisely tell everything about you. It might even tell certain aspects of your personality, which you were not aware of, with the help of this aggregated data.

Till now, we may haven't realize the fact the machine knows us better than anyone else.

More than humans, we are all now the walking and talking databases, which can be used, misused and abused, based on whose hands it reaches.

Well, like every other technology, it can have both negative and positive aspects. We would focus more on the positive aspect of Big Data in this chapter and how it is the fourth pillar of true digital transformation.

Insurance and Banking

The insurance industry can make good use of this available data and personalize the policies for its clients.

Normally, in small towns, almost everyone knows each other. There is a family doctor, a person who had information about your grandfather, father and other member's medical history. So it is very easy to make a personalized insurance policy based on this data and offer proactive advice.

But in big cities, with a large population, making personalized insurance policies is not possible by human beings. It's very difficult to collect all the data related to citizens and process it.

But now, with availability of Big data & AI, machines can create 'personalized insurance policies'.

Similarly, the senior bankers know our liabilities, assets, shop turnover, children's marriage or education, and can offer us personalized advice in terms of loans and payments.

Retail Sector

Big data, with AI, has been integrated in major retail companies across the globe, and spectacular results have been witnessed so far.

With the IoT sensors placed across the entire space to capture all the unstructured and structured data, things have become quite seamless in tapping the user behavior.

The shopper's footfall data is well-mapped with the area/section where they spent most time along with the duration. This provides valuable estimates to the retailers and helps them decide where they should be investing further.

Advanced analytics, when applied to this big data, can be the decision-makers in the marketing strategies of any retail company.

Medicine and Big Data

In the medical sector, this Big Data can be a valuable asset when it comes to devising a new vaccine or a treatment. We can expect data analytics to guide our Corona warrior researchers and doctors to test the vaccine with the help of this Big Data, as discussed in the IoT Chapter.

Newer devices are invented to keep track of this data and keep the consumers aware of the health indicators, how many calories they have burnt, the number of steps they've taken or the duration of their exercises.

Several research studies, government reports, Electronic Health Records, smartphones and wearable devices are sources of this big data. The medical fraternity has made the best possible use of this data to turn it into an actionable model.

Fit Bit activity tracker and Apple Watch are classic examples of the resultant innovation of big data. These devices keep a tab on our physical activities and give exhaustive reports on health-related trends. We can optimize this data and make use of it. The data is sent to cloud servers. The servers, as we know, are connected to the physicians responsible for maintaining our overall health and wellness programs. Similarly, various apps in our smartphones like HealthKit, CareKit and ResearchKit monitor our health activities and keep us updated.

This big data has supported the medical sector in new diagnostics, cost-effective treatments, medical research and preventive medicines.

MORE DATA is Better

Machine & underlying algorithm become better with more data. Hence, companies are looking for more and more data, *i.e.* Big Data to achieve real transformation.

Earlier, the companies, which grew or became big over a period, were forced to spend more on hiring managers whose sole job was to monitor tasks, reduce waste and break the communication silos among different layers of their respective organizations. Growth always came with a cost back then.

But in this age of Digital Transformation, we can produce more with only a fraction of the original cost and this "More" helps us create new "Value" in the following ways:

1. With Artificial Intelligence, machines become smarter if we provide more input data.

2. All networks and platforms become better if more players join that platform. Here the value multiplies with big data.

So now you can provide personalized experience & scale the model.

In my opinion, Kodak's downfall was not exactly caused by Fuji or the advent of digital photography. Mr. Steven at Kodak came up with a digital camera, using which photos could be captured as files of stored data and later be displayed on computers.

But getting these photos from "Digital Camera" still required lot of work. This involved, lot of friction & there was no instant gratification.

With Smartphones, it was very easy to click 'many photos (in various poses)' & see them instantaneously.

Also, Social media apps like Facebook and Instagram created a new habit in the users, that is to share those photos anytime, anywhere with anyone…immediately.

Earlier, we used to click photos, only during special occasions like marriage or a birthday party. Clicking photo was not a daily activity. It was reserved, only for special occasions.

But, with the arrival of Smartphone (to click photos, anytime, anywhere) & social media (to share those photos/images with anyone, immediately), created a new possibility for the customer.

This was a new "Value" for users as now they could share any experience like travel or day-to-day work with more photos and on-the-go.

This value creation with the fraction of extra cost in our smartphones and social media apps like Facebook and Instagram have caused real disruption in many business models across the world.

So in my opinion, Smartphones & Social media was the real cause for the downfall of Kodak.

Travel Industry and Big Data

Travel industry also embraced these new technologies and has shown immense progress here.

Ever felt more personalization and customization in the travel packages than earlier? It's like the other person or the travel portals know the nitty-gritty of our visit to a particular city or a country. This is the result of the input data we have provided to the travel advisors to chalk out a smooth travel plan, designed only for us.

The entire hospitality industry has been integrated under one roof with the help of big data and it can give us intelligent travel solutions for our next trip. The regular flyers need not worry now because the machines have already learned their travel taste and frequency, and out of nowhere they delight us by sending random discount text messages that are tempting enough to plan one more travel!

Here are the areas where big data has intervened to digitally transform the travel industry:

- Checking the occupancy rates, booking status in the various preferred hotels and suggesting the best option.
- Mapping the spending and purchasing power, and suggesting more personalized packages.
- Critical information about travel plans like weather uncertainties, flights and upcoming events in the touring city.
- Knowing the trending travel spots across the world and keeping us updated on the same.
- Handling our billing and payments in the travel plan.

- Automated promotional travel messages to loyal customers, based on location and data.
- Giving a fair competition analysis of our rival travel company.

During this COVID time, everyone was itching to travel & stay in a 'Safe place'. Bingo!!! Check the internet. You will see lot of travel & hotel options, which are near your city & where various safety precautions are already put into place.

During this year's Christmas long weekend (year 2020), almost all big resorts near my city (Bangalore) had a 100% occupancy rate.

Also, information was available for not 'So Safe' hotels.

In case, one was planning to travel by car from Bangalore to Mysore, there were certain APPs/website, which were showing data related to - where to take break/eat food during this road trip.

So, if we are technologically updated, then big data can plan our entire travel itinerary and leave us surprisingly delighted.

Final Words

We can very well say that big data can be referred to as the fourth pillar of digital transformation. Hopefully, we expect this data to bring in more trends in the future and fresh innovations to make lives easier.

Data management has made decision-making in the business very easy. We no longer have to assume and make business plans based on our whims and fancies. They are now substantiated with data analysis. This process has made risk analysis easier, and business management a transformed process.

All this structured and unstructured data has once again proved with its innovative ways that the customers remain the kings and businesses need to reinvent their ways of working to maintain their unrivaled status. With more awareness and technology in hand, the customers can sway the future of a business anytime, based on their preferences. So, it is good to know their preferences based on the BIG DATA!

In the end, I would conclude the chapter with this historic quote by Marissa Mayer, Former President and CEO of Yahoo:

> *"With Data collection, 'The Sooner*
> *The Better' is always the best answer."*

CHAPTER 9

DIGITAL ANTHROPOLOGY: TECHNOLOGY AND HABIT TRANSFORMATIONS

Anthropology is defined as "the scientific study of humans, their behaviour, and their societies in the past and present patterns."

- **Cultural Anthropology** is the study of human culture, which includes their norms and values.

- **Linguistic Anthropology** studies how language influences the social life of humans.

- **Digital Anthropology** is the anthropological study of the relationship between humans and digital-era technology.

"These Definitions are taken from Internet"

Let's try to understand the impact that digital anthropology may have on our overall evolution (including our thought process & various habits)

I will first take a simple example of electricity here for understanding anthropology & human habits. Before electricity came, our daily habits were different. There was nothing like 'nightlife'. Just think of city like Las-Vegas, without electricity.

So, the arrival of electricity has changed our habits & hobbies. We can very well say that human race evolved to the next level, after electricity came.

I will say that, Digital will have the same impact here. That is, human race will evolve further because of various new habits, hobbies & change in human behavior due to digital.

Has this digital transformation changed our behavioral patterns from a societal, linguistic and cultural angle, and if yes, then how? We will look at the various aspect of this transformation here.

Digital Transformation and Privacy Behaviors

Let us take the example of some social media platforms like Facebook, Instagram, Twitter, and OTT APPs. We observe some interesting and strange behavior patterns here.

This digital transformation in social media has brought strange changes in our behavior. On one hand, we are demanding our family members' privacy to be a part of individual consent; simultaneously, we also involve strangers to watch our private life content on different social media platforms. No doubt, social media has given the privacy to watch, create and share individual content. Ironically, despite the privacy settings, it has exposed an individual to a huge outside world by showcasing his/her timeline.

Earlier, no one was comfortable sharing their photos or family photo albums in public. Now, we show and share each moment of our lives on Facebook and other social networking platforms.

Privacy settings have created strong boundaries between the significant others. It is no longer considered ethical to peek into someone's content irrespective of relationship equations. The right to privacy is an important buzzword.

I have even observed that the teens many times demand that their parents should knock the door, before entering their own kid's room.

As children enter their teenage, they start demanding privacy and separate rooms.

Today, four individuals of a family often watch different, customized and independent content, unlike the earlier days.

During the times of Mahabharata and Ramayana serials on Doordarshan, cricket matches or watching "World This Week", the TV technology integrated the entire community.

During my college days, there used to be only one TV for the entire hostel. So, we all used to sit together and watch TV. There was no other option of watching different movies or TV serials or entertainment programs.

Things are just the opposite today.

Now, each student has his own smartphone. He can watch, whatever he wants, on his smartphone.

Earlier watching two movies in a week was a luxury. Now watching one movie daily is normal. Now, a new value/demand has been created by smartphones & OTT APPs. If you notice carefully, smartphones & social media has created these new habits amongst us.

Unmet Demands

Earlier, the family members, living in a one-bedroom set, could not watch different movies as there would be only one TV in the house. With digital transformation and the arrival of OTT APPs, many people can watch movies as per their choice, at their convenient time and on their mobile phones. The unmet demands are getting fulfilled with this transformation.

Visibility

There is a transformation in an individual's visibility quotient here. Being visible online has become a requirement today. Everyone flaunts their lifestyles on a platform like Facebook without a second thought. It's the reflection of the same behavior, which we practiced in our small group of 'significant others'. This 'significant others' scale is now broadened to thousands and hundreds of unknown friends to flaunt our new dresses, jewelry or a big house. Instagram is all about lifestyle image-sharing. The more the followers, the more it is linked to one's self-esteem. As per a study, the excessive use of this technology has been linked to a similar effect induced after taking drugs.

Mini Celebrity Status

Technology has given celebrity status to every individual by providing a customized platform for their profiles on Facebook and Instagram. It was a privilege earlier to have an individual account to express personal opinions and preferences. Now, we are all mini-celebrities and are quite opinionated about issues around society. It might look insignificant if seen at an individual level, but if you look at it from a nation and society's perspective, it has a snowball effect. It has the potential to bring revolutions by integrating all these individual opinions. We are hyper-connected now.

Selfie Culture

The selfie trend in photography has given rise to narcissist tendencies in individuals. We are no longer dependent on someone to click pictures for us. Even if there is someone to click, we prefer selfies. In my opinion, there is nothing wrong with clicking oneself, but it is an indication of the increasing individualistic culture. India, recently, witnessed the highest number of selfie deaths in the world.

We have seen many cases, where to get a 'Perfect Selfie' or 'Sensational picture' (which can be posted on Instagram), people have clicked photos, while hanging from high-rise buildings or from the cliff of a mountain.

Smartphones are selling like hotcakes based solely on the selfie features; they have become as important as dialing and receiving a call facility.

To emphasize my point, our earlier generations were not having these habits (Clicking Selfie at dangerous places, in dangerous poses..). But for young generation, this 'new' habit is 'almost normal'. Nothing wizard about this…Really!!!

Has the Transformation Connected Us?

My house help, who can't write, can create videos on WhatsApp and shares it with us. So, I feel that we are connected. At the same time, we have also observed that our families, while eating food, are gazing into their smartphones during dinner. So, I seriously wonder whether smartphones and digital transformation have connected us or created distances?

The Workplace Scenario

Now let's scale its effect to the professional level.

Earlier, bosses had secretaries, who were good at typewriting. The best skill of these personal assistants was to quickly type an error-free content/letter as the bosses dictated. This has now been replaced by computers.

We might see the next transformation in a way wherein bosses will talk, and the speech-to-text converter will convert their speech into a letter. This way, secretaries can focus on other meaningful core works.

If you take a look at your organization, consider the new or the young crowd. They are always hooked to their smartphones and have cultivated new digital habits in no time. This observation about digital transformation tells us that we also have to adapt to this new culture at our workplace. If we don't do it, we may lose members from senior management because they might work on the basis of their old habits.

This is why the human resources department is finding it challenging to bridge the gap between the new tech-savvy generation and traditional upper management. The youngest intern in any company is much more tech-savvy than Gen X or Gen Y Boss. They no longer type the message and send it. The simple voice command saves much more time. Good editing software can correct grammatical errors in the speech. Suddenly, the need for typewriters seems to have vanished, and the roles are adapted into more intelligent ways of managing the responsibilities.

The younger generation is not daunted with testing new technologies and adapting them into their ways of working in the professional spheres compared to the wise old management. HR must now create a platform where old wisdom and new technology associated with each other for better workplace efficiency. It will, otherwise, be an issue of conflict management and attrition for HR. Start-ups give more exposure to the new generation for learning and development regarding new ways of working.

Final Words

In brief, I would like to mention here that, with digital transformation, we are witnessing new behavior among us.

These changes are like a double-edged sword. If they give us some 'never-before' privileges, they also add new responsibilities. We are responsible for taking this transformation in a direction that can give us more power and privilege.

By understanding Digital Anthropology, we can safely conclude that the study of the relationship between humans and digital-era technology, helps us to understand how human society is evolving using digital technologies or getting impacted by digital transformation.

CHAPTER 10

DIGITAL ANTHROPOLOGY: INVOKING THE SUBCONSCIOUS MIND

Leading psychologists have proved that our minds have two sides-the conscious and the subconscious.

As Sigmund Freud says, "the conscious mind is equivalent to just the tip of an iceberg and it is the subconscious that is the storehouse of all the memories, desires, and feelings."

Our conscious mind is very rational and mostly concerned about the logical things in life. It is a reservoir of thoughts, memories, feelings and wishes that are very much a part of our awareness at any given moment.

Let us take an example of the subconscious mind. Suppose we learned swimming or cycling in childhood and have not practiced it for years; we still know how to cycle and swim. Our subconscious mind has registered it and retrieves it whenever we resume those skills.

In ancient times, our Saints & Sadhus used to do Samadhi (Deep state of meditation). In my opinion, by this Samadhi, they were able to control their sub-conscious mind. By invoking & controlling their sub-conscious mind, they were able to attain peace, cheerfulness & happiness (even though, sometime, the atmosphere around was chaotic).

Here's another example. We often do strange things when we are in love with someone or when we listen to our favorite music. This is the time when our subconscious mind takes over our rational thoughts or conscious mind. The subconscious mind plays a very big role in the way we behave. It can retrieve the oldest memories and desires if some related experience can invoke it.

We are talking about the subconscious mind here because digital transformation has not just altered our habits temporarily but has made a deep impact on our subconscious minds.

Technology has been successful in invoking our subconscious desires and transforming our behaviors at deeper levels. Digital technology can now tap our minds to know our habits, desires, likes and dislikes.

It has been proven that even drugs invoke our subconscious mind wherein our rational behaviors take a back seat and we end up doing certain actions that we would not have done while being in a fully conscious state. Yoga and other meditation techniques can teach us how to control our subconscious mind. It takes a lot of effort to control this subconscious mind.

We cannot allow our subconscious mind to rule over our rational thinking in our daily-life. There has to be an apt balance between the conscious and subconscious mind for a balanced lifestyle.

Almost all digital companies use the AI algorithm and big data to invoke our subconscious minds. They observe the patterns of our likes, dislikes, spending and consumption, and then frame a customized marketing policy based on this intelligence. This is where machine learning steps in and observes what our subconscious mind desires at the deeper levels.

Following this assessment, strategies are customized based on these desires and likings. They show us exactly what we like to see. Sometimes, this might surprise us as to how well these machines understand us!

We may want to see what we like during the recreation time; the subconscious mind gets active during the recreation period. So, the activities like watching movies during weekends are now totally customized for us by ACID.

All these integrated technologies generate stronger algorithms for the machines. The more we switch through channels, the more data we provide to the machines and the stronger it becomes at analyzing and providing recommendations.

There is likely to be a stage wherein the machine would have learnt the concept called 'You', and 'You' have now been trapped in their marketing strategy. 'You' are now totally addicted to this like a drug user.

Machines know the real 'YOU". In many cases, even you, yourself may not have realized some facts about yourself.

Based on your spending patterns or eating habits etc., it will tell you that you are careless about your health or you spend too much on fancy cloths.

Also, machines now control the subconscious mind, which, in turn, has started trusting this machine. Now the machine will show what it wants to show us.

So, first you see what you like, later you start liking, whatever is shown to you.

Machine has fully understood your sub-conscious mind & it shows, whatever you wanted to see....a vicious cycle.

Many successful companies, including FAAAN companies, are now trying to influence your sub-conscious mind.

As explained earlier, we are now 'developing' new habits.

1. Taking Selfie at dangerous places,

2. Not knowing your apartment neighbor but creating friends on social media & chatting with them long hours (Even though you may not have met them, even once physically)

3. Gazing into your smartphone while driving

4. I have many friends, who just keep on checking their social media status/mails, even though they are on vacation with their family at beautiful beach.

We can take more examples in this context.

Netflix is the classic case to explain the idea of employing Artificial Intelligence and tapping the massive database of its preference. They produced an in-house series like 'House of

Cards' and get a blockbuster response from the audiences. They would have first researched the users' choices, likes, dislikes or I must say they would have played with our subconscious mind by showing us a particular content and tapping on the response.

All these OTT APPs (Netflix, Sony, Amazon Prime..) are creating a taste in us for a certain kind of content, based on our subconscious mind's desires.

Facebook gives us friend recommendations depending on our saved contacts or by email, in our smartphones. The good thing is that one day our lost best friend from childhood could send a friend request, and our joy would know no bound. We don't get tired of thanking Facebook for this artificial intelligence. Simultaneously, let's say a person has clicked or watched a particular brand advertisement. In that case, it will likely show him more such content, making its algorithm stronger with this fed data by the person's use of the social media platform.

Let's take the example of Amazon/Flipkart. If you have bought the same company's shoes twice, it is most likely that the section will show you something like this- People who bought this also bought this or similar shoes.

YouTube: If you have been watching a particular event or show over a specific period, technology would have already guessed that you like the celebrity. In no time, it will show all the possible movies or songs related to the particular celebrity. Then the advertisers slowly start attaching the other contender's videos tempting you to look at them. You might start liking them sooner or later.

Machines play well with our subconscious mind and manipulate our choices without us even knowing or realizing it.

And we enjoy watching these shows, thinking a miracle might have happened! It's not! It's just that machines have overtaken your sub-conscious mind.

Personally, in my case, I love to listen to music and songs. Based on my listening preferences, one fine day, YouTube suggested the music of Vangelis (1492- Conquest of Paradise). I must confess that it was heavenly music and I couldn't have got the albums of Vangelis if YouTube had not suggested it. Post that, it suggested songs of Mexican singer 'Guadalupe Pineda' (Historia de un Amor song). I don't know Mexican, but the music and voice were a treat for my ears.

Just think of it. There must be millions of songs and music composed till now. It would have been an almost impossible task for me to listen to those songs, which are so mesmerizing and suits my taste of music; just because of the related 'videos' I get to hear the music that was created a long time back in some other country, and in a different language.

Let me give some more examples.

Shoe manufacturer, Nike, makes sure that it invokes a core belief of staying healthy. Once the belief is reinforced that health is the most important thing, they anchor this concept with their shoes and other digital products.

Google search results are not the same at two different locations.

Try this with your friend. Both of you give some key word to search on Google.

Now, based on the location & online preferences learnt by algorithm, it may generate different results.

Drug-Like Addiction- Digital Addictions

Addiction is a condition in which a person engages in the use of a substance or behavior for which the rewarding effects provide a compelling incentive to pursue the behavior despite detrimental consequences repeatedly.

As per my opinion, the reasons for this kind of addictive behavior can be any of the following:

1. **Instant Gratification:** Suppose we post something on social media platforms and receive a response within hours. We love it and crave more for such immediate responses. This is exactly what drug addiction does to us. It provides instant gratification.

2. **Intermittent Positive Reinforcement:** Our minds are highly susceptible to these forces. Various apps use these hooks in terms of the 'Like' button. How many times do you check that and get a "Wow" feeling? Or wait for your "likes" to increase?

3. **Drive for Social Approval:** We all give importance to what other people think of us. Suppose many people click the 'like' button, we would certainly feel good. In the same way, the lack of positive feedback creates stress.

So, now my question is, how many digital apps have you downloaded on your device? My friend gets 86 notifications from various apps! And he gets glued to checking and responding to them. This is exactly what I call "Digital Addiction".

Final Words

Personalized content is an exceptionally good thing, but in my opinion, you must be very careful while entering your personal data into these machines. We have seen many examples proving that machines use our data to strengthen their algorithms and get intelligent. It has both positive and negative implications.

Do not blame technology for this addiction and changed habits. It is entirely up to us to decide how to use it. Every time we engage with these devices, we are exchanging one of our most precious things-"Our time". Let's spend that time with our families.

We have witnessed a big debate of-how machines can take over our work. A lot of books and articles have been written around that.

My firm belief is that a Machine can have a Mind but will never have the sub-conscious mind, which a human possesses.

Before the first industrial revolution, humans with strong physical bodies were in demand.

Post Industrial revolution, work, where a lot of physical labor was required, has been replaced.

Later, humans with sharp and rational minds were needed.

On a similar note, in the last few years, machines can do work, which could have been done by the conscious human mind.

But as I said earlier, machines will not have sub-conscious mind.

In the coming days, humans who have good control over their subconscious minds will win. Human race evolution will happen, around the work, where skills and work related to human subconscious minds are required.

Some are trying to achieve this by doing mediation & Yoga. Even I believe that by doing YOGA properly, you can control your sub-conscious mind.

Some people call this state as "Mindfulness" or 'Deep Work'. Others say that skills related to the sub-conscious mind like empathy, emotional intelligence will help.

As detailed in the last two chapters, in coming days, our evolution (habits, hobbies, daily work routine…) with be driven by our sub-conscious mind.

And digital anthropology will be the key to understand human subconscious mind.

CHAPTER 11

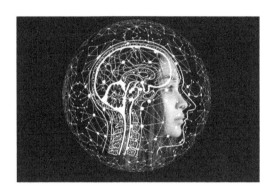

DIGITAL ANTHROPOLOGY: ARE YOU READY TO CHANGE YOUR BELIEF SYSTEM?

Digital transformation has changed the ways of doing business and led to our transformed ways of working.

In my opinion, the real success of technology should be to smoothen our way of working. It should make our work simpler, smoother and more efficient. If it doesn't, then real transformation has not arrived at all in the major strata of society, economy and politics.

As discussed in earlier chapters, our sub-conscious mind plays a major role, in what we believe in, how we work, what we enjoy, how we behave…

Unfortunately, we are still in the same mode of equating Hard Work with Success. The advent of Artificial Intelligence, along with IoT and Cloud, will ensure that the success parameter is no longer measured in terms of the number of hours spent working. Now, technology has brought us to an era where work is about innovation and creativity.

Hard Work = Success… ????

Before technology arrived, working hard for long hours was considered efficient, especially in the industrial and manufacturing era. We have heard stories of many 'heroes' who worked for long hours. It was a mental model created to believe that it was a sin if you were getting money without working hard. Only kings or rulers had this privilege of comfortable living. So, there was a demarcation that the ruler community had leisure time and the working class was supposed to slog. Everyone, therefore, sang the praise about being busy and working hard.

Technology has brought us to a stage where we need to rethink and change these hard-wired beliefs I have mentioned below:

1. I work hard;therefore, I am.

2. Working long hours is good. We should slog 60-80 hours per week at our office.

3. Our work is our identity. Who we are is tightly linked to what we do.

4. If we are not successful, then it's because we didn't work hard. Suffering and sacrifice are the key moral markers of success.

5. Getting big money without toiling hard is evil money.

6. Read 'Productivity Improvement' books. These books will tell us 'How to be stress-free' to squeeze that extra hour in which we can do some extra work.

7. We can and should do multi-tasking.

Creativity Is the New Hard Work

Remember, now we are living in an age of a knowledge economy. Creativity and innovation are important here. The routine and repetitive works are already being handled by technologies, namely, IoT, Cloud and Artificial Intelligence. We need a proper system to work here. Upcoming technologies will demand a more human approach to assist their operations in a controlled way.

Let's replace our old thought process & hard-wired beliefs with the thoughts mentioned below:

1. Creativity requires downtime and relax mind.

2. Don't measure how many ideas one has created in a day.

3. Productivity is about predictability and this doesn't fit well with creativity.

4. The busier we are, the less creative we will become.

5. Don't suppress emotions at work. It's okay to cry, weep or shout.

6. Creative thoughts appear when we least expect them and are difficult to force on the spot.

7. Don't force the mind to switch between the tasks. Focus on one thing at a time.

So, in your company, if you want to break the silos at all levels to bring the real digital transformation, don't put Gen Y through rigid working hours. It would be best to give them the flexibility, space to express themselves and question their seniors (the rulers). As leaders, we have to create a fertile ground where seeds of ideas can grow. Don't expect them to put in nine hours of work within the four walls of the office.

Collaboration In Your Team

We live in an age where a sheer competitive spirit is not enough to take us ahead in our career in the long run. Our collaboration skills are equally important. As we have already seen, money can never be the 'forever' motivator in our career; many other factors matter in the working space.

One such belief that we must instill in our organizations is teamwork or collaboration efforts. One day, the new technologies will take such a powerful shape that they will seek for many heads to guide them in the right direction or else they might take the direction towards destructiveness.

In almost all big companies, one of the major issues is that various departments or team members don't talk with other department members or in other words, there is no teamwork. To validate it, I have a crazy idea.

The HR may not agree with me, and it may be labeled as data privacy. Let us peek into the employees' official email and check how many official emails an employee sends to his manager or direct reports vs the mails to other team members. You may be astonished to know that employees may often be sending multiple e-mails to the person sitting next to them but belonging to a different department. How many internal issue escalations are happening through e-mails? How many mail chains are going on, with more than five persons in CC?

Technology understands much more than we can anticipate. Now, with NLP (Natural Language Processing), we can even get data on the sentiment of the official e-mails like:

1. How many emails employees are sending to other department personnel, praising their work?

2. How many emails contain gratitude or empathy?

3. How many of them contain negative emotions?

If there are too many issue escalations or cross-department emails, it may indicate that the team members are not working together.

So, we will have to train our teams to understand that gone are the days when they had to compete to bring excellence as a value addition to the organization. A collaboration streak has to be instilled to reshape the future.

Workplace: A Breeding Ground of Ideas

A change in our habits is required in the workplace as expectations have also undergone a 'change'. It's no longer the company that decides whom to hire. Gen Y wants to be a part of the decision on whether or not to work in a company.

The hiring trends are also changing now as the game is in favour of the employees. We no longer see the culture of loyal employees who used to spend decades in an organization. The breed of employees, who used to join and retire from the same company, is vanishing now. Gen Y looks for cultural changes in an organization, linked directly to their 'new' ways of working and thinking.

The senior management is still caught in the traditional ways of working and cannot provide a fertile ground for youngsters to innovate and think in new ways.

Final Words

Start learning, 'how to un-learn'. And don't be afraid. You are not alone, who is going through this turbulent journey. Changing 'deep rooted belief systems & human sub-conscious mind' is not easy. But now, this is surely required. True digital transformation will demand a positive change in our belief systems. And a clear understanding of 'Digital Anthropology', will surely help us in driving this positive change in our mindset.

CHAPTER 12

LEARNING ORGANIZATIONS, AGILE AND DIGITAL TRANSFORMATIONS

For a true digital transformation, we must ensure the process of learning and unlearning happens at the same time.

If we look at the constantly changing technology, the management, and the employees' relative mindset, there is a huge gap in adopting the new technology.

In earlier chapters, I had discussed about Industrialization, Instant gratification & hyper personalization.

We had also looked at WISE problems, before you can apply ACID formula.

I have also discussed about digital anthropology & why it's difficult to change our sub-conscious mind. A change in mindset is required.

So where & how to start?

In my opinion, your starting point should be the creation of an Agile Mindset & Learning organization.

Both of these requires, 'Fail Fast, Fail Forward, Learn Fast & Scale fast' culture.

You will not be able to fail fast if you are not 'DOING AGILE'.

On Similar lines, a learning organization requires a constant feedback (learning) loop.

Both, Agile Mindset & Learning Organization, are per-requisites of the Digital transformation journey.

The Arrival of Agile

Agile is a collection of principles used in software development and project management. Agile focuses on enabling teams to deliver work in small, workable increments, thus delivering value to their customers with ease. Evaluation of the requirements, plans, and results take place continuously. This helps the team in responding to changes in a quick manner.

Internet Source: What is Agile: Understanding Agile Methodology and Its Types (simplilearn.com)

Till now, most of the organizations had followed the Waterfall Model earlier. This model is a breakdown of project activities into linear sequential phases, where each phase depends on the deliverables of the previous one and corresponds to a specialization of tasks. In this project management activity, the software development activity was divided into different phases, and each phase consists of a series of tasks that has different objectives.

If we go by the industry trends, the Waterfall Model is almost dead, however, due to the fixed mindset and old ways of thinking, the traditional organizational environments and processes use it even today. Many organizations call themselves AGILE, but they are still in the mode of the partial waterfall and partial AGILE. Experts term it as the AGILE FALL Model.

In this case, we work in Agile, but the main work is delivered at the last moment only.

If you are embracing AGILE in the digital world, you have to allow small failures.

Let me give an example here.

Suppose you have two systems, say system AB and System CD, assuming both are imperfect systems and go down from time to time, AB goes down once in two days, but it surely comes up within the next ten minutes whenever it goes down; system CD goes down only two to three times in a month. But you do not know how much time it will take to recover when it goes down. It can take between 2-40 hours before it comes up. Now, which system is better?

If you measure how many times the system goes down in one month, then the system CD is the winner as it goes down only 2-3 times a month. But if you measure the total system uptime, then the system AB is the winner. It is predictable and provides more uptime.

I have seen many examples, where a company claimed that it is following AGILE. But the whole delivery happened at the last moment only and a buggy software code was shipped. Due to various escalations from client's side, senior management (who had seen the Waterfall Model), called for 'usual' root-cause analysis of this.

And guess what, conclusion of this root case analysis was almost the same as any other root cause meeting, done may be 20 years back. Conclusions were:

1. Use a new tool for extra code validation or tweak the existing tools for tighter control
2. Find out new Process Control ideas
3. Plan a Knowledge Transfer session for team members on new and latest topics

I will suggest that, you should also check in your office, whether root-cause analysis meeting are happenings and what are the conclusion.

If you are really following Agile, then your team must be continuously delivering MVP (Minimum Viable Product) on a continuous basis.

Your team must be learning on a continuous basis. If you are delivering one big project after say 6 months than surely you are not doing agile. You have not created the environment for AGILE to succeed.

In my opinion, the majority of our team members want to do good work. They don't want to ship buggy code, but they need an environment where they can 'Fail Fast, Fail Forward, Learn Fast & Scale Fast'. They need adequate time to do productive work. You must check where your developer is spending time today.

As a software professional, I can tell, only 30% of their time goes towards productive work. The rest of the time is spent waiting for requirements, design clarification, the work area to be ready and preparing status reports for management review.

Avoid the time spent unnecessarily. Your team members should be able to spend 70-80% of their time coding and designing.

I have seen that in many organizations, team members are not doing work, as per their core strength. That is, if you have hired a person to do coding in JAVA, check, how much time, he is really spending in coding.

Before COVID, many of key team members were supposed to travel, meet clients etc. Yes, that is important. But whether your key team member should spend time doing travel arrangement, booking hotels, preparing for VISA etc.

You can give secretaries to your core team members. Let them spend time on activities, for which they were hired for and in area, where they are real experts.

On similar lines, secretaries can do fantastic work in various admin area, as they become expert over a period of time.

I believe this will be win-win for all.

AGILE is not about using new tools and following new rituals at the workplace like daily stand-up and customer interactions. These tools should help you in achieving nimbleness. If not, please question, why you are using these new tools and these daily rituals.

It is not easy. It surely requires a change in mind-set. But don't get into the intermediate model of Agile- fall (That is you start doing small waterfall projects, in the name of AGILE).

"The main aim of 'agile' is that you should always have working software and you should be able to demonstrate your software to the customers, take feedbacks and improve it in real-time. It should be routine work rather than 'once-in-a-while' process."

Having understood Agile, I will suggest that we should apply the underlying concepts in our digital transformation journey also. So, let me rephrase the main aim of agile for our digital transformation journey.

"Our transformation program should be executed in such a manner that we should be able to review the progress on a daily basis by demonstrating the 'real value' which has been created. We should be able to take feedback from all stakeholders and improve/modify our execution plan in a real-time basis. It should be a routine work rather than 'once in a while' review.

It would be best if you don't do this transformation just to one corner of the organization. This transformation should be applied to each and every area of the organization - Marketing, Pre-Sales, Sales, Product Development, Product Implementation, Purchase and Billing, HR and partners. All segments of organizations must be involved in this transformation programs.

Benefits of this transformation program should reach the entire cycle, including:

- All the internal team members of the organizations.
- All existing customers for an existing product.

  Do value addition by lowering the cost, faster time to market and better turnaround time.

- New value to new and existing customers.

This transformation will be like an orchestra, where all instruments are played in harmony; it is needed, but we have to decide how this orchestra has to be played while executing the transformation program. We must keep these two important things in mind - not all instruments should play at the same time and we need to bring both synergy and harmony to an event.

Each department is likely to have a different level of understanding when it comes to 'Agile Mindset & Agile Working'.

So first, assess the maturity levels of different departments and teams, then, create a baseline, following which, decide how you will execute the transformation at all organization levels.

This process will need an extensive breakdown of the horizontal and vertical silos of the organization.

What is your opinion? Have you re-defined your team's goals for this holistic transformation, which is both harmonious and synergetic?

Making a Learning Organization

Most employees in an organization are opposed to change. It becomes difficult for them to unlearn the old ways of working. In the process of learning new technology, one must be ready to unlearn the old one. This is the hallmark of a learning organization.

As per Peter Senge's book, 'The Fifth Discipline', a learning organization facilitates the learning of its members and continuously transforms itself over a period. This is one of the best books on disciplines that I have come across. I fully second the ideas of Peter Senge when it comes to transforming an individual or an organization through his principles.

To drive the digital transformation journey, you need to create a Learning organization. This will help you & your team, in overcoming your 'old deep-rooted beliefs'.

As per Peter Senge, a learning organization, must have:

1. **Personal Mastery:** We should learn continuously in our areas. We must be aware of our incompetence and be open to feedback on our work. If you really want to become a master in a subject, you should be open to get brutal feedback about your work & should be happy to incorporate the same.

2. **Mental Models:** This refers to the deep-rooted bias in our minds. We have stereotypes and mental models based on gender, age, etc. We often generalize and assume about the people around us. We start making decisions based on that pre-conceived bias. A person, who wishes to be really transformational, will be self- aware and self-reflect on these biases before judging someone.

3. **Shared Vision:** As it is said, the heterogeneity in a team can be a big value addition to the combined thought process of a project. A shared vision should be built along with the team. When a diverse team shares its views on a project, the team's overall IQ increases, and many valuable inputs can make the process transformational. Do not dictate from the top. Let the communication flow transparently.

4. **Team Learning:** As we have discussed, the team's collective intelligence is always more than the individual's sum. So, the transformational process is a process to learn together.

5. **Systems Thinking:** In a big system, it is very easy to pass the buck due to the highly bureaucratic structure. We all are a part of the big picture. Before blaming others, think how your actions may have impacted others.

Peter Senge portrays an example in his book. If you visit a hotel and decide to use the hot water from the tap there, it might happen that when you open the hot water tap, the hot water gets dispensed after some time. If you don't know this, you will open that tap fully and suddenly get a gush of hot water. Then, you will have to quickly close this tap and open the cold-water tap. So, in this case, chaos is created due to your lack of awareness. Now, you must not blame the hotel for this. You have created this chaos. It would be best if you had opened the tap and waited for some time rather than blame the system.

Final Words

To become a true learning organization, we must educate ourselves on business as well as life, as learnability is not just required in an organization, but it is a virtue worth cultivating in real life.

So, let's create a learning organization & apply Agile Mindset to drive Digital Transformation.

CHAPTER 13

DIGITAL TRANSFORMATION: THE POWER OF NETWORKING

Digital transformation has a foundation in the power of networking. Any good technology not reaching the masses have no value irrespective of how great it is.

Our innovations must find a utility value among the masses for their complete usage.

One important factor behind this process is the power of networking. You must have heard that.

'Your Network' = 'Your Net worth' now.

Such is the power of networking for real digital transformation.

Chat with my friend SAI

The other day, I was talking to my close friend Sai regarding this process and we had arrived on this.

Sai: Do you know who has been the biggest salesperson?

Me: Yes, the person who sold the first phone.

Sai: Really?

Me: Yes. The customer, who bought the first phone, had zero value with that instrument. The value got added only when others also bought the phones. The first phone piece had zero value. Today, when each human being and each entity is connected, we can say, 'Your Network is your Net-worth.'

Sai: Okay, so you are talking of Uber, Amazon and Airbnb.

Me: Yes. In my opinion, we still have many areas that are left to be explored where.

Network + Innovation = Big Value.

Let me give you an example of a t-shirt company, 'Threadless'. This t-shirt company held a design contest which was open for all. As a marketing strategy, it decided to print the t-shirts only with the most popular designs. In this case, there was no need to hire artistic talent. The young and enthusiastic members participated to gain recognition and win prizes. As the marketing team, they only did the 'word of mouth' publicity and told their friends to buy the t-shirts. It is an example of a great network, connecting all stakeholders.

Digital Community

Digital transformation, at its peak, has the potential to make our lives smooth so that we don't need an asset in the future. Considering the way digital transformation is disrupting the business models and our lifestyle pattern, the day is not far when owning something might go out of trend.

I call this 'Digital Community'. Community, where groups of people are connected with each other & share various utilities.

We all know the models of Uber and Airbnb, which do not own the assets, yet are involved in the assets' business. Business models like these were unimaginable some years back, but now we are in the age of digital disruption and witnessing a seismic shift in business leaders' thought processes.

This digital community concept or the networking concept will transform both our personal and professional world.

For example, in an apartment, Digital APPs can help the resident of an apartment to share washing machines, dishwashers, etc. There will be no need to own this asset.

A digital community can be formed in an apartment, which can help in sharing various equipment or assets. Also, the users will have the provision of rating the services,*i.e.* the people who have rented the equipment and those who have borrowed the equipment. This will be a good guide to the other members in the future.

Similarly, we can create a Digital community for lending money. This community can be used for P2P (Peer to Peer) lending, crowd funding of loans, etc. We can on-board the start-ups that need the money and other High Net Income professionals to fund them.

Like UBER and Airbnb, the digital community has a massive database of users harboring the potential to bring about such futuristic solutions in terms of owning an asset.

Three Tips for a Powerful Digital Community

1. **Friction-Less Entry:** In my opinion, don't charge the stakeholders during on-boarding. No value is created just by joining a digital community. It would be best if we charge only after a successful deal happens through this digital community or else the stakeholders will be hesitant to join the digital community. We must encourage more stakeholders to join and post.

2. **Content Curation:** As joining is free, non-serious players may also become a part and put off the serious ones. It will be a tough job for them to find a suitable partner from the crowd and keep them away. So, we must put some smart algorithms which quickly connect the correct buyers with the sellers. We should also publish the rating, the activity details of all players, like the number of interactions done by each player, and the number of deals successfully closed. It will create transparency and visibility and more people gain trust value in their respective community.

3. **Stickiness:** Publishing various players' history also discourages the buyers or the sellers from finalizing the deals outside the digital community . Our digital community should help in post-deal activities like disbursement, payment schedule, delay, default and overall tracking.

Are you also creating such a digital community through your products or services? Is your company a part of some network near the customers? Are you able to provide a 'multiplier' effect to your customers?

In today's era, we can't win by 'Price effect' where we offer low cost or discount or say by the 'Brand effect,' which requires deep pockets. We have to focus on creating our digital community. We have to make a credible digital community that trusts us on our proposition that this newly-arrived technology can create a difference in our lives and has the potential to make our operations smooth. All in all, it will make our lives easy. If we convince our digital community members about the technology's credibility, it allows the frictionless entry of suppliers and consumers and curates the exchange of value between them.

Over time, each new member in the digital community increases its value in a non-linear way and makes the entire digital community transform digitally.

In the end, my final words would be a quote:

> *"At least 40% of all businesses will die in the next ten years... if they don't figure out how to change their entire company to accommodate new technologies"*
> **–John Chambers,**
> *Executive Chairman, Cisco Systems*

CHAPTER 14

WATCH OUT
FOR THESE THINGS

Undoubtedly, Digital Transformation has reinvented our thought process, business prospects and our personal lives. As per a report, global digital transformation will be a major investment area for organizations worldwide with the spending potential expected to grow from $6.7 billion in 2017 to $417 billion by 2026.

So, Digital Transformation is a huge game to watch out for. But as every technology and transformation has a flip side to it, Digital Transformation is no exception. These are some of the issues, which we should watch for.

Security Issues

We envisage a future where we will be hyper-connected via our laptop, bank systems, airports, TV, phones, security cameras, mobile phones and power plants. Our sensitive information is lying all over the virtual space. If someone needs to play around, the information is easily accessible.

Let us consider the post-COVID-19 scenario where we have accelerated the pace of digitalization since the majority of us are working from home and are connected through digital platforms like Zoom. We are sharing sensitive corporate and personal information over these digital platforms which can be a cause of concern in terms of our security. A lot more work is happening over phones, video calls and chats. My question is -can someone accidentally share the company's confidential data over the network?

To keep the country's economic activity going on, we might be taking the help of robots in various places to automate the work. This work can be replaced by robots in bank branches, shops and airports; we will see robots' advent, doing a lot more work. This will avoid humans contacting other humans, and a sanitized robot can do the work much more efficiently. Now, this is the beauty and the mantra of digital transformation. But what happens, if someone hacks into this, the whole system can come down in no time.

Cyber security will be of paramount importance. Various medical devices will be connected through Wi-Fi. Can someone hack and create a problem in a medical pacemaker attached to a patient?

There are chances that suddenly many computers start accessing the same websites and bring them down, by increasing the traffic. It is DOS (Denial Of Service) to genuine users.

One can play havoc by playing with the software of self-driving cars and streetlights.

Environmental Impact

As per the United Nations Report, e-waste is growing rapidly due to this digital transformation. It was estimated that 40 million metric tons of e-waste were discarded in 2014, of which 7 million metric tons were from the 2 big countries alone. This implies that we throw almost 800 laptops every second.

The landfills are getting mounted by this e-waste releasing volumes of toxic chemicals into the environment every day.

We need to devise ways in which we can recycle these digital products and save the environment.

Virtual Identity

As discussed earlier, with the help of ACID, you can now create the full persona or a person's virtual identity with all his or her data, including biometric. The data can reveal startling bits of information.

GDPR (General Data Protection Rule) has come into the picture in Europe. It is a rule by which the company has to take consent from the customers before using or sharing their private data. Since the law is still in the inception phase, there is still a big chance of some companies misusing it. There is a high risk that anyone can use our personal or private data to hack or manipulate our minds and behavior to run a smear campaign.

The probability of the misuse of Virtual Identity increases a lot in this case.

Also, as our data and habits are shared (one can find out, which places, one has travelled in the last week, whether he has parked his car near a liquor shop at night…discotheque…).

Be careful, now, this data can be misused.

Fake News

In today's overloaded information age, it is very difficult to identify and separate fake news from real. In the US, we need to say-'I will tell the truth, the whole truth nothing but the Truth". This is true especially in times of elections. A smear campaign can be run based on half-truth and twisting the facts as per the situation's benefit. Spin doctors can quote or misquote to reveal only a part of his/her conversation and use it to their benefit. Earlier, we were not connected, but now, we are hyper-connected. The bad news about someone can travel faster than our imagination and permanently damage someone's reputation. I still remember waiting for news time on the radio or tuning to the BBC for authentic and validated news. Now, there are so many news channels and social networking apps and websites from where fake news can spread fast and create huge problems in our society that could lead to riots or changing election results.

Digital Transformation and Employment Cuts

With the advent of smart sensors and Artificial Intelligence, a lot of speculations are going on about future work. A survey estimated that more than half of the global population worries about losing their jobs due to this transformation, which will automate almost all the processes where humans are involved.

We can say here the newer roles and responsibilities will emerge, and the employees can be redeployed to higher levels and jobs. Every technological revolution has seen such phases, but we can carve out higher human roles with the right adaptability and skill.

New Emerging Roles in the Digital Transformation Era

We will be witnessing new roles in the digitally transformed era. The combination of ACID (Artificial Intelligence, Cloud Computing, IoT and Data) will transform major roles and responsibilities in the employment sector. The IoT sensors and Artificial Intelligence will take over manual, repetitive work. Humans will be involved in work that will require human capabilities not to be tapped by machines that include creativity, collaborations and management.

The following roles will emerge in the coming times prominently across all the employment sectors:

Data Scientist

The role of the Data Scientists will be one to watch out for. We will need two types of persons —one, who owns the robots and, other, who can work under them. The Data Scientists will help in running the software applications and make out the What, When, How and the Why of data.

Customer Experience through Story Telling

We all love stories. People who can understand customer requirements can narrate or relate the product to customers. They will be in demand.

Sentiments and Empathy Manager/Chief Joy Officer

Persons, who have real empathy, connect and understand the customers' problems, will be in demand.

We need these people in hospitals. The machines will scan all data, compare them with tons of previous data from similar populations/patients, and suggest the diagnosis and cure. A human will always be required to talk with the patients and explain them personally.

Chief Community Officer

People, who can think and come out with a way on how a company's work will benefit society, will also be in demand. The companies might end up harming the society or environment around it. These people will ensure that the distance between the haves and have nots is reduced. They will help in peer-to-peer communication and people and community management. They will also make sure that all company decisions are ethical, and there is no bias.

We will need the following futuristic humanly skills in the automated world:

- Soft skills and EQ will be better rewarded than certification and IQ
- Cognitive flexibility
- Judgment and decision-making over routine data-scanning abilities
- Creativity and critical-thinking skills

Final Words

ACID technologies should not scare us or make us apprehensive about the future of the work. We must start thinking on the lines where they play the roles of our intelligent assistants for a smooth life.

Remember the old saying:

> *"Technology is a useful servant*
> *but a dangerous master."*
> **Christian Lous Lange, Historian**

I want to conclude my analysis with a saying of Jeff Bezos; it emphasizes that Digital Transformation is not a luxury anymore but a necessity. If we do not adapt to the new changes, we will soon perish as many legendary companies have vanished over time.

"There is no alternative to digital transformation. Visionary companies will carve out new strategic options for themselves—those that don't adapt will fail."

The correct usage of technology decides the status of a master and a slave. Make the technology serve you better than yesterday and invest that pending energy in evolving more as humans and not machines! I would close all the thoughts with this quote.

> *"The real danger is not that computers will*
> *begin to think like men, but that men will*
> *begin to think like computers."*
> **Sydney Harris (Journalist)**

CHAPTER 15

THOUGHTS AND EXAMPLES ON DIGITAL TRANSFORMATION

Linkedin has been a platform that connects like-minded professionals. This is an excellent platform to brainstorm ideas about the progress, challenges and development in the employment space.

I have always been an active LinkedIn user. Whenever I share my professional ideas, they receive good inputs on my thoughts on Digital Transformation and other work-related topics.

It is a pleasure to share them with you through this book.

Let me put these topics one by one here for your inputs and become a stakeholder in this thought journey.

(1) Robotic Process Automation (RPA)

Use Robotic Process automation, wisely.

Sai: Hey, do you know that we are now using RPA in our bank?

Me: Really? Great to know that.

Sai: Earlier, our staff used to take out the physical print- outs of the customers' account statements, fold them, insert them in envelopes, write addresses on them and send it for further mailing processes. Now, everything is automated and no manual intervention is required.

Me: Wait a moment! Are you still sending the physical statements by post? Why don't you just e-mail the account statement on customers' registered e-mail ids? Have you checked with them? After COVID-19, the customers will also prefer emails rather than physical account statements.

Me: Any more such developments in your banking system? Sai: While filling various application forms for customers, repetitive data was being asked at multiple places. Now, the users have to provide this data in just one place -and the tool populates the data.

Me: But I have observed the same data is asked multiple times despite having all these tools even now. You must re- design these application forms. This is not "a true Digital Transformation". We are still using the same traditional ways of working.

Sai: So, how do I start this kind of Digital Transformation in our system?

Me: You need to review, streamline the current system and processes, and start it NOW.

(2) DIGITAL TRANSFORMATION–Start Now

Sai: In my bank, we have started Digital Transformation in a big way. Our management is planning big investments in new technologies.

Me: Good to know.

Sai: We want to provide banking services on all channels and devices.

Me: What's your definition of a channel?

Sai: Banking through the Internet, Mobile, Smart Watch,

Me: Channel is just a context. By context, I mean the place, time, person and devices involved in Digital Experience, but the most important part is applying empathy while providing the solution or service.

Sai: Really?

Me: Let me give you an example. I went to the USA last year. I had taken a pre-paid travel card and travel insurance from my bank and gave them all the details of my tour.

Sai: Okay!

Me: I had given Credit Card (CC) details in the hotel, while checking in, and the bank still declined my transaction. It was nighttime in India, and, no one from the bank picked my call.

Sai: Then?

Me: I waited for a long time and, somehow, contacted a bank representative. He told me that my credit card was being used in a different country at an odd hour; the system had declined the transaction to avoid any frauds.

Sai: What could have been done in that case? Me: They could have done two things here:

1. Travelcard, Credit Card and Insurance teams are separate groups in the bank. They already had all my travel details but did not share them internally.

2. Someone from the bank could have called on my registered phone number to check and help me out in this case.

This was the classic case of Silos existing in the banking system despite having all the tools of Digital Transformation. So, I am still not convinced about Digital Transformation happening in the banking sector despite having all the conditions set for transformation.

The same discussion led to my shopping experience in the USA.

(3) Improving the Shopping Experience in Brick & Mortar Shop with Digital Transformation

Sai: So, how was your trip to the USA? How was your shopping experience.

Me: It was good, and I did a lot of shopping there. I went to all shopping malls like Target, Walmart, Kmart, Sears, Sam's Club, etc.

Sai: Great. You must have enjoyed it a lot!

Me: My kids gave me a shopping list that included exotic or exclusive things; it was hectic. Moreover, all these are huge shops. After the office meetings and work hours, I only had one hour left for shopping. I wish I had a digital app to help me out there. It could have guided me.

Sai: How?

ME: An app that I can download (it could be the shop's Exclusive Digital App) on my mobile which could guide me further for the items I was looking for. This app could show where the goods were kept. An app on which I can type and which helps me navigate and suggest an optimal path. Also, it should show similar items and any discount offers in case I plan to buy more things. Since I was in a hurry, I had to ask the staff for each item. They were helpful, but I was still running around. All the items in these shops have bar codes, which can easily show the live location and the items' availability on a digital app.

(4) Innovation: In COVID-19 Situation

Me: Usage of ATMs has been declining in the current situation as people are moving to digital payment methods.

Sai: Ok, I have heard a lot about that. But, to be honest, though I have many digital payment apps, sometimes I still need cash to make payments to the local vegetable vendors or grocers. What will happen if ATMs are not there?

Me: Let me tell you about a cool innovation. This is related to 'Cash Withdrawal, done by DBS bank & SOCASH". They have tied up with various merchant shops. You can open your account with DBS Bank and download SOCASH APP. When you require cash, enter the details in that APP and a QR code will be generated. SOCASH app will help you find you a nearby shop that is part of this network. You can go to that shop and show the QR code to the shopkeeper. He will scan the QR code and give you cash. This is a 'win-win' situation for all.

In this way:

1. Banks can reduce the physical space required for setting up ATM centres and save on rent.

2. Since the shopkeeper gives you cash, he need not worry about the security of excess cash/need to deposit excess cash in the bank.

3. Customers have many shop options to withdraw money. Further, there is no need for them to use the keypad of ATM machines.

I think SOCASH will offer this service in association with other banks as well & DBS will also roll out more such cool innovations.

(5) Avoid these Common Mistakes in the Process of Digital Transformation (DT)

Sai: As part of DT, we will be moving to a new "ABC" system.

Me: Ok. What is required for this transformation?

Sai: Some functional changes are all that it takes. Also, we require 60 reports to be developed.

Me: Will these reports be sent to end customers or regulators?

Sai: No, these reports are for internal purposes.

Me: Just curious. No data is being compared in these reports; say the product sales from last year to this year or profitability from last year. Why do you require these reports?

Sai: Um…

Me: These reports should help you in taking some action/ decision. It should tell you about the products, which are not doing well. I don't see any of this data in these reports.

Sai: You are right.

Me: Earlier, most of the things were manual. Maybe during that time, banks wanted these physical reports to preserve it safely. Now, everything gets stored on the computer as a soft copy, so why do you still require these? To harness the power of digital technology, re-look and re-define your data and processes. Also, in your current system, a lot of duplicate customer Ids would have been created. Remove those duplicates. Only then, it will give you a full view of the customer. The new system will not help unless you re-define your existing thought process.

(6) How AI should become my IA (Intelligent Assistant)?

I am a regular user of Netflix, Kindle, Amazon and Banking apps. They give me a good personalized experience, instant gratification anytime, anywhere experience, but one thing is missing. They use past behavior and context to render this experience.

My banking app understands from which city I am doing my banking transaction, the time(day/night) and the mode (mobile/laptop/watch). However, it still doesn't know my mood while I do the transaction. When I visited the bank personally, my Relation Manager (RM) knew exactly whether I am frustrated by some banking service, complaining or in a happy mood to discuss further investment plans. Based on this input, the RM would greet and plan the discussions accordingly.

The same is true for retail shops also. The shop owner is able to see my face and body language to decide whether I am in a bad mood or joyful so that he can engage me in long conversations and show and sell the new brand of dark chocolates, maybe.

This is where I believe AI will play a big role. What am I typing or what is my tone when I speak? Will AI in Alexa determine these factors: whether I am happy or angry? Will it just do what I say or give me suggestions also?

I am waiting for the time when AI will be my IA-the Intelligent Assistant!

(7) Digital Transformation (DT) in Bank…What will the customer Get

In this conversation, I tried to understand from Sai's perspective how Digital Transformation in Banks would help customers in the future.

Sai (S): How DT in banks help?

Me (M): Banks will get a single view of customers and save cost by automating.

Sai: Wait. Banks will gain a lot. But what will I gain as an end-customer of a bank? I already use its online and mobile banking.

Me: How do you invest in stocks? Sai: through 'ABC' Wealth Ltd.

Me: How do you pay phone bills?

Sai: Digital Wallet

Me: How do you book air tickets? Sai: I use 'ABC' Trip APP.

Me: How much did you spend at the hotel during family dinner?

Sai: I don't remember.

Me: You don't remember how much you spent and how you spent (cash, banking app…)

Me: What is your bank a/c number? Sai: I don't remember.

Me: After DT, the bank will give you an Id SAI_2210 (if you were born on 22nd October). There's no need to remember the account ID.

Sai: Cool

Me: Do all transactions through this ID. Your bank will maintain your spending pattern and create a new segment, ONLY FOR YOU! After DT, bank will provide you services, totally personalized for you.

Sai: What's the catch?

Me: No catch. The bank is saving money, which earlier, they were sharing with others. Now the bank has your exact spending pattern. They can create a lending/deposit product as per your exact need. No need to buy pre-defined deposit/lending products. It's win-win for both bank & you.

(8) Success-Personal and Professional Life

This post was about knowing what you mean by real success and measuring and creating it.

Sai: What is success?

Me: You must read Simon Sinek's books.

Sai: I haven't read. It will be great if you can brief me about it.

Me: So, when do you think you can call yourself successful in life?

Sai: I will be successful once I have a big house, car, millions of dollars, have travelled to 20 countries.

Me: Really? Think again. Would you think the same during your old age, with relatives and friends not talking with you or if you are ill with no cure?

Sai: Oh...

Me: Both in your personal and professional life, you always play an infinite game. There are just no defined goalposts. Sometimes, you will know WHY you feel happy after doing a certain task. And post that, you can pursue your 'WHY' to remain happy. Of course, you need a certain amount of money to fulfill basic needs and then pursue your 'WHY.' There is no definition of victory here. In life's journey, you have to be successful for "N" years, and no one knows the value of "N". The same is true for a company. A company's founder must have started his organization with a clear "WHY" like "To give more computing power in the hands of the common people, create a fancy/dream-like place, which can be enjoyed by family".

To achieve that 'WHY', let's say a company was created for producing computers, better software and fantasy parks. The company can be profitable for some years, but the teams need to pursue their 'WHY'.

If you want to feel real success, find the "Why of Your Life" and create new success parameters.

(9) How Digital Engagement will Change Our Shopping Habits & Spending

Many of us use Amazon Online for our weekly shopping, which is 'Shop & Ship'. First, we shop on Amazon Online and, later, those goods are shipped to our homes. I bet that this will change from the 'Shop & Ship' to the 'Ship & Shop' model. It has already started happening in some cases like BB Instant (from Big Basket), which has installed vending machines in our society.

Amazon is continuously collecting data related to our monthly shopping preferences and habits. During summer, we may order more juices. During winter, our preferences are likely to include personal care products for rough skin, more sugar and other related ingredients to make sweets or snacks during the festive season, instant soups, etc. Amazon collects data for each member based on their shopping habits, which could include an upcoming celebration in the house like the birthday of kids, marriage anniversaries, etc. Amazon must have collected all this data for each household, who knows?

In the future, there is a high probability that Amazon will start sending those 'seasonal items' to us along with our normal grocery items. The eCommerce giant will first ship these items (without you explicitly ordering) and the delivery person will leave all those items at our doorsteps. Now, if we keep those items, only then our credit card will be charged or else there may be 'Returning boxes/trucks,' in which we can drop those items that are not needed.

Let us consider another case. If you have been regularly buying your monthly grocery items from Amazon Online, and it happened once that while ordering, you searched a particular brand of chocolate and it was not available, maybe Amazon will ship some other brand of chocolate to you as a compliment. In the future, if you like this, you might start ordering that particular brand's chocolate regularly. Quietly, your shopping bill will start increasing, but you may not mind it!!!

I simply love this innovative model. What's your opinion? That's how the digital world will pamper us in the future.

(10) Is Your organization A Digitally Transformed Organization?

A digitally transformed organization is the one that offers you anytime, anywhere availability.

It should give us a 360 degrees view, Instant Gratification and Personalized Experience.

Let me suggest an experiment here, which you can do at your company.

Give the following points for each question:

10 – Highest

1 – Lowest

The following are the parameters.

System Silos

To know how the organization works, find out how many systems your employees have to use, to complete normal official work. You must include all the systems on which the employee works, apply for the leave, do the travel booking and approve the purchase order. Are these systems available on the CLOUD, which can be accessed 24/7 from anywhere?

You get 10 points if it is only one system.

Data Silos

As a Manager, find out how many systems you need to touch to get a full view of your employee, including his or her work, salary details, overall work experience, his strength areas & areas of improvement etc.

You get 10 points if it is only one system.

Instant Gratification

Find out whether each employee can devote full time for the work in his core competency. How much time is wasted in the waiting process, it could be getting requirement clarity from different departments? How much time an employee can devote to coding in software development and how much time he is waiting for the build to get completed?

If the answer is "No wait", fantastic, you get 10 points.

Personalized Experience

Find out whether the changes are done in policy or system to incorporate individual aspirations or needs. If you really want to usher into transformation, your company's policies (appraisal system, training system, communication structure...) can't remain the same as last year.

These policies should keep on getting modified & upgraded, at-least on a quarterly basis. Looks too frequent......Remember, you have promised your customers, instant gratification & zero friction. So, your employees should also get instant gratification!!!!!

So how much is your score? Not good!!! Let me suggest a solution here. (And there can be many more....)

Identify two 'Inside Out' and two 'Outside In' parameters, which are most crucial to the business like the product output, cost, time-taken to implement the product, cost saved, or new business offered for customers.

Now, establish a system, by which an automated report can be published, daily for these parameters. (No manual intervention, please...)

Publish it on a common platform without any manual intervention.

This whole exercise will help you in understanding the deep-rooted SILOS in your organization & will help you in breaking the same. Also, it will bring transparency in the system.

(11) Leadership Dilemmas

This post was about taking tough decisions in a badly hit economy. As a leader, what strategies can one make to keep things afloat? It is a war-like situation, and I took the lessons from a book by Jocko Willink and Leif Babin.

In the army, the teams stay in remote areas. As the chief of the army group, you become good friends with all your team members; they become your family. Now during any military operation, you have to send some of these people to fight. For a mission to be successful, you have to send your best soldiers to fight out there. You don't even know whether they will come back or not. This is a big dichotomy. To win a battle, you have to send soldiers who are dear to you, knowing that they may never come back, but you have to take those hard decisions.

Even in civil life, we face situations like this, especially when economy goes down.

There can be three options:

1. Retaining all team members with full salary, but in this case, an entire company may shutdown one day because of the lack of funds to run it.

2. Identify some team members and tell them to leave. We may have groomed them, but it's the time to take the call. This will help other employees to get salaries.

3. Tell everyone to take a salary cut, but then your bright team members may not be happy as they may be compensating for others.

So which option, you will take?

(12) Gratitude And Success

We all feel that the grass is always greener on the other side. You must be thankful for what you already have. Let me make it clear with the age-old story of a goat.

Imagine that there is a field full of green grass. There are many trees in the field, and a goat is tied to a tree with a rope. The goat has three options:

1. It can stand at one place and eat the grass right there.

2. The goat can cover the area and eat the grass within the limits or till where the rope allows.

3. It can stare at the other part of the field and think "I wish I could have them"; the grass is greener on the other side.

What do you think is better behavior here?

Circle around, eat and enjoy what you have or crib that the grass outside the circle is better? There may be a few obstacles when the goat circles around. For instance, some stones may be there. The goat can always push it. Don't worry about what will happen if the goat has already eaten grass in one area. More grass will soon grow. Maybe next time, better quality grass will grow. It all boils down to APPRECIATING what you already have and DOING what you surely can do. Frustration and obstacles are always part of any game, but you will win if you have passion, a learning attitude & gratitude. Instead of cribbing, be thankful of what you have.

(13) Stockdale Paradox

Jim Collins has referred to Stockdale Paradox in his book "Good to Great". This is named after Admiral Jim Stockdale, a US military officer held captive for eight years during the War.

He was tortured brutally yet Stockdale never lost faith during his ordeal:

"I never doubted that I would get out, but also that I would prevail in the end and turn the experience into the defining event of my life, which in retrospect, I would not trade."

Now, look at the paradox here.

He noted that it was always optimistic of his prison mates failing to get out of it alive. They were the ones who said, "We're going to be out by Christmas and Christmas would come and go."

Then they'd say, "We're going to be out by Easter." Many Easters passed and they died of a broken heart.

What the optimists failed to do was to confront the reality of their situation. Stockdale approached adversity with a very different mindset. He accepted the reality of his situation. He knew that he was in crisis, but he stepped up and did everything he could to lift himself and the fellow prisoners' morale. We must retain faith that we will prevail in the end.

We must confront the most brutal facts of current reality. Stay Safe, happy, healthy and we will win.

(14) Artificial Intelligence

Here are some insights into one good use-case with an unconventional model and why AI is a hot topic.

This technology has created a wave of discussion more than ever before, in terms of its proliferation and usage. It can sway in any direction based on its use. It can be the biggest boon or bane. The use cases are already there to prove where AI can take us in the future.

Sai: Why AI has become a hot topic now?

Me: There are three reasons why AI is having more use cases and is a hotter topic to discuss in terms of upcoming digital transformation.

1. **The Big Data:** The more the input data, the better the simulation of the human mind. It is due to the availability of a lot of structured data-documents - and unstructured data like videos and conversation data that provides ample scope to make the machine intelligent.

2. **The** arrival of Reinforcement Learning has increased the competitiveness in the software market. We have much-enhanced software algorithms today and cheap hardware for big data storage.

3. **Cloud** and Network of Networks: In this hugely interconnected world, everyone is connected across continents. Everyone can assess data or a product from anywhere, anytime because everything is available on the Cloud.

Now there is enough connectivity to tap on the data required to be analyzed by AI.

One of the best examples of this is ALEXA . Based on our shopping habits, we get good recommendations on Amazon.

Based on our movie watching history, Netflix displays/ recommend movies.

Let me tell you one interesting use case of the latest fashion clothing. How do you apply AI here? Remember, as this is related to 'latest' fashion trends, you can't use old data (what was fashionable in 2019 is not fashionable now).

Sai: So, what can be done?

Me: In my opinion, you can do the following:

1. Create a data model based on a customer's browsing/ shopping history in other areas (like house décor). Also, it would help if you considered the gender, time of the year, and weather conditions.

2. If you are thinking of new creative clothing (colour, style), look for it in other industries.

3. Habits and trends on social media.

What's your opinion? What else can be done here?

(15) Making a Difference

I have expressed here as to how changes in the banks can lead to a transformation across an entire nation and wish to be a part of this change. Here's a small talk between me and Sai on digital transformation in banks.

Me: I want to bring about a difference in the World's economy.

Sai: Don't talk at the 1000-feet level. Give details.

Me: The banking system controls every country's economy.

Sai: How?

Me: In every country, the business owners get loans and establish factories that produce goods/services. They either sell these products within the country or export them. Thus, they earn money, create employment, and influence the economy.

Sai: Still 500-feet!!

Me: Banks collect the deposits and lend that money as a loan to business owners. The interest gained on these loans is the banks' profit. So, if I can reduce the cost of maintaining the deposits and the cost of giving loans, banks will give cheaper loans, which will help set up new factories and help the economy. I want to bring about a digital transformation in the banking area.

Let's list down the differentiators in this process.

1. Remove redundant systems and processes in a bank. Use the CLOUD and reduce hardware costs.

2. Use Analytics to reduce the chances of loans becoming Non-Performing Assets (NPAs).

3. Reduce the cost of transfer of money between two parties. Reduce credit fraud, as well.

4. Reduce interest on deposits by giving a personalized deposit facility. One can deposit and withdraw money anytime, anywhere and use any channel for any amount. Sell a structured product at a low cost.

(16) Cool Technologies-Blockchain... Don't run behind each shiny object

Many of us jump on to learn the new technologies in the market as soon as they spring up. My friend Sai also had the same plan. I asked him about the reasons for learning about new technology.

If you ask me, I would say you must know the core value of any technology before jumping on to learning it because everyone is doing the same. Do not follow the herd mentality.

Sai: I am learning Blockchain. Me: Why?

Sai: It's cool new technology!!

Me: So, which business problem are you planning to solve through Blockchain?

Sai: Oh...I can use it anywhere!!

Me: Blockchain only helps you create the "Temper Proof" platform, which is visible to all or a group of users.

Sai: So, I can use it for payments.

Me: Remember that as Blockchain offers a temper-proof platform, you will not be able to do reversals. You have to put another transaction to do that. Are you ok with it?

Sai: Umm, I never thought about it.

Me: According to me, you should use this in big-ticket transactions like Trade Finance, Loan Syndication, Land records and Customer identity. In these cases, once you have created and verified the record/transaction, you don't want to temper the record.

Remember, we use a distributed ledger concept here. That is, for a data block, the hash is generated. That data-block hash value is used in the next data block and a new hash value is created.

Now all these data blocks are stored at various nodes (say at five nodes). So, if someone tries to temper data, he needs to change all these hash blocks as well as change it on all the nodes.

If data at one node is different from the other four, it will easily get detected.

Sai: Okay.

Me: You may not require a similar feature, say, in retail payments. It can be overhead.

In retail transactions, you may want to do a reversal or backdated payment. This will become very costly (in terms of maintenance and slow system response) in the Blockchain platform. Solve correct business problems.

What is your opinion on this? What is the core value of the Blockchain?

(17) Ambition vs Capability

There is a huge correlation between your ambitions and capabilities. Let us know how.

Case 1: If Ambition > Capability- You remain hungry, but you may be able to handle the future.

Case 2: Ambition < Capability-You are satisfied and remain where you currently are. Will you able to handle the future?

Do you know your capabilities? Do you know your ambitions?

What will you choose?

(18) How To Build a Winning Team?

Have you noticed a strange thing in your organization that 70% of your team members feel that their performance is above average (as a team's performance)? Think of it. It's mathematically not possible. Team members can be good but 70% of your team member can't be above average of the overall team.

If that is the case, then it is the time for deep engagement and discussion with your team because it is logically impossible. It denies the performance curve of an organization.

What is your view?

(19) Future of the Work OR Work of the Future

This clarifies the doubts that futuristic technology will take away our work. It might work in a very different and pleasant way.

Sai: This Digital Disruption is different.

Me: The previous disruption was different too. In digital disruption, humans are required to give expert opinions while working along-side machines (M/c). That's what I call Augmentation.

Sai: No, now M/c will be analyzing tons of data and predicting.

Me: Sai, some of these were true earlier also. Sai: Really? Give me an example.

Me: Do you trade in the stock market? Sai: Yes.

Me: For stocks, we do technical analysis and arrive at 'Candlestick patterns', 'Moving Average Convergence Divergence', etc. All these are based on past price patterns of stock. This has been there for a long time, still, traders and financial planners are needed.

Sai: Ok, what about human sentiment analysis?

Me: That also was there, though I am sure you had never faced this!!

Sai: Umm…

Me: Look at the Lie Detector Test. It is based on different types of questions; Machines look at the pulse rate change in facial expressions, heartbeats and give results (whether you were lying or telling the truth). But remember, it's only a recommendation. The human jury/judge takes the help of this data before giving a verdict.

So, now the value of human opinion will go up. We will be able to make better decisions. The reason is that machines must have scanned all relevant data quickly and accurately.

(20)How The Digital World Will Spoil Us In The Future?

Recently, I was searching for a movie called "Boiler Room" on NETFLIX. This movie is based on the stock market. Though Netflix didn't have this movie, instead of saying 'No result found', the search results showed titles like Wall-street, The Big Short; these movies are also based on stock market.

We have seen, several examples like this, earlier also. For instance, while searching for a product on an eCommerce portal, once we get one item, the results will start showing up more items one can buy.

But in this case, data is shown for the items that are not part of the Netflix library. It means, Netflix not only maintains data of similar nature movies in one place, but it also stores data of the movies, which it does not have but which are of similar nature. Wow!!!

(21) KINDLE Experience

I have already discussed it in one of the chapters as my thoughts on Digital Transformation.

- WHAT remains the same- We are reading books.

- HOW part has changed-We are buying online.

- WHY this has happened-Because we all are looking for Instant Gratification, Personalized Experience, Cost-effective Experience, anytime and anywhere.

One of the 'WHY' is now the consumers start looking for service/experience without necessarily buying the underlying asset. Uber is a fantastic example of this. We wanted a travel service with good experience, without buying a car.

Netflix has started creating 'Netflix Original movies/TV series based on customers' viewing habits.

Here I have a suggestion, which I want to share with you all.

I still have to buy books on Kindle, though I want to read it only once. Though Kindle Unlimited provides a library to rent books, it is for limited titles. My question is why can't I download unlimited titles by paying an annual fee? Also, for fictional novels/books, Kindle has enough readers' data. They know what is selling in fiction. Why not create a Kindle Original Fiction novel?

(22) Creativity and Technology -3 Key Points

Sai: How was the book Creativity, Inc by Ed (Co-founder of Pixar)?

Me: Simply, Wow. Sai: Really?

Me: To me, Pixar is the best example of creating a culture where

"Creativity + Technology = Wonders in terms of Animated Movies"

For a movie like 'Toy Story,' you are the creator of various characters. You imagine/tell how TOYs will talk, cry, express various emotions.

Sai: Three key points, please. Me:

1. People are your greatest asset. Hire people who are smarter than YOU.

   While hiring, give more weightage to 'Potential to grow' rather than their past work. Create fertile ground for them. Allow them to decorate their working place. The workplace should be filled with emotions and energy. Make interdepartmental interaction necessary. The 'Development, HR, QA, Business team' sit on different floors in many companies; how will they naturally mingle with each other? Encourage cross- pollination of ideas.

2. Company's communication structure. It should NOT mirror its organizational structure. Managers should not feel insecure if problems related to their group are discussed in common without speaking to them.

3. Don't focus too much on preventing failures. Build a culture of how to Recover and Learn from them. Encourage problem-solving skills.

(23) Digital Transformation - Augmented Reality (AR) & Virtual Reality (VR)

Sai: I found a way to record my night dreams. Me: How?

Sai: At night, I will wear a smartwatch and put on AR/VR specs. These specs will send signals to the smartwatch. All my dreams will get recorded on my smartwatch.

Me: Ummm!! But this is not what AR/VR does.

Sai: AR adds or provides details about a real object. With AR Spec/AR App, you can get more details about a historical building like when it was built, and by whom? Suppose you go to a new city. It will give details about important places, shops or in factories about each machine-their status, maintenance need, etc.

VR helps you in getting immersed in a virtual world. So, once you wear VR spec, you see and experience a different world.

Till now, VR is mainly used in entertainment, but after COVID, I can think of more use cases for VR. Many times, a client wants to visit the vendor's factory or office before signing a deal. Now, vendors can create a VR App to detail their campuses or machines. A client sitting in the USA can get a virtual tour of his vendor's office in India. He can virtually touch the walls, rotate the machine and get a 360-degree view of the full campus. VR can also help in online education by providing a virtual tour.

(24) Digital Transformation - The Key Points

For a complete DT, you must keep these ten points in mind.

1. In your company, plan digital and IT conversation together.

2. Often, there is an inverse relationship between a vendor's maturity and the ability to innovate.

3. Any product built on cool new technology will require big support cost in future.

4. Companies have to start valuing a culture that builds off failure.

5. The power-point is not so powerful now. CIOs need to communicate with digital products.

6. Please market the value and not the activity.

(25) Digital Jugaad

We are undoubtedly spoilt for choice. In the last few years, many 'Digital Products' especially smartphones with new apps and cool wearables have made their way into the markets. The target audience of many of these products is the middle and upper class. What about the bottom of the pyramid section? I see a good market potential here. Have the habits transformed in this section as well?

A few people from this section are using current technology and putting a Jugaad to meet their needs. Here are a few examples.

My maid is illiterate and can't type. But she uses WhatsApp to create an audio clip of her status (in case she cannot come for work) and sends the same to us.

A few days ago, my car underwent a small accident. My driver created a video of "the engine/other damaged parts of the car" and sent it to me for my confirmation before taking it for servicing.

My driver has a bank account and access to online banking which he is afraid to use because the bank website is in English and he cannot read or write. What about having an app, which can listen to his instructions, confirm back on voice, and then actually execute the transactions?

Like this, there are many other websites, which take written English instructions.

Taking a cue from this, I can see a big market here. There is a huge market for new apps that can listen to the instructions in native languages, translate the same into English and get that service done. It will have the inclusion of the whole society into the Digital World.

(26) Benefits of 5G - Four Customer - Friendly Use Cases

Post-5G-rollout, data streaming will be very fast. So you will be able to download heavy videos in few seconds.

1. As of now, Uber and Lyft send text notifications, with driver and car numbers.

    Going forward, they can send small video notifications. This video can contain a real-time image of the car's driver and details (shield details between the driver and the passenger). It will help in identifying the car and give passengers more confidence in terms of safety.

2. When you get confirmation details, the restaurant can send a video, showing real-time images (as well as COVID-19 safety measures, which it has been applying).

3. If you are reading a book on a digital device, a small video can be embedded. So, once you are on page 10, a small video plays (this is not the link to a video that you are forced to click today). The video just plays once you are on page 10, and you can switch off. Authors can convey their ideas through videos also.

4. In the bank statement, when it shows spending details, it can also display an image/video of shops where your Credit Card was swiped. The bank already has these details. It will help you in reconciling back. These bank statements can be made more interactive.

(27) Digital TRANSFORMATION - Key Points for Leaders

Leadership plays an important role in Digital Transformation. Here is what I think the leaders in any organization must focus on:

1. Are you spending half of your time with the business?

   Check and make sure that your calendar reflects that.

2. Plan a business strategy for the digital world.

3. Transparency is a two-way street. If your team is willing to show you the correct data, you should have enough patience to see that. The correct data may be bitter but don't shoot the postman. Hear this & encourage this culture.

4. To drive a change, you need to start it from your end. This May require throwing your ego out of the door. Check whether the team members (not in your reporting line) come to you for suggestions. If not, you are only a positional leader.

5. Your decisions should be data-driven, but your team should not spend two hours preparing that. You promise instant gratification to your customers so your own internal systems can't take endless efforts to get data.

6. Encourage your team to learn new things. Don't worry that if they learn new things, they will leave your company for better jobs. Worry about what will happen if they don't learn new things and they stay in your company.

(28) Going Digital - Social Score

Sai: What is this 'fair play award' in IPL?

Me: This award is given to a team that plays the game in the right spirit. Teams like Chennai had won the main tournament as well as the 'Fair Play Award'. The same concept can be introduced in our lives for a better society.

Sai: How?

Me: Smart devices connect everyone. We can assign a score to an individual based on his conduct on a real-time basis, and it can be stored at a commonplace. If a guest behaves properly during his hotel stay, he gets some points. If a taxi driver drives properly, he gets positive points. Based on various interactions/ posts on social media, the score for a person can be arrived at.

Sai: What's the use?

Me: If you are checking into a hotel and your score is higher, you need not pay any advance. Also, the hotel can give incentives to guests who have a better score. This will help them to advertise that their hotel is 'Family-friendly'.

Just the way a credit score encourages good financial behavior, this score can also encourage overall good social behavior of a person.

An overall score can include your behavior with your neighbors, children, elders and maids... your contribution towards the environment. It is a win-win for an individual as well as society.

(29) Your phone knows more about YOU than you know yourself

Let me take an example from my personal life to explain this. I asked my friend Sai to give me access to his phone.

Me: Hi, Sai. Please give me the phone on which you watch movies. I will explain to you how technology knows the real 'YOU'.

Sai: Oh? Very interesting. Take this phone; all my apps are installed on this device.

Me: Sai, It looks like you love watching Sci-Fi movies. And why have you ordered these types of soaps and perfumes?

I thought you don't like such things.

Sai: Oh! It seems like you can get to know quite a lot about me from my phone.

Me: Yes. You must be careful. By going through various apps and data, one can figure out "Real You" and your preferences in terms of movies, songs, books and more.

Sai: I never imagined that technology could let others know so much about me. Now, I can understand why these apps keep showing me movie and shopping recommendations that could interest me, probably.

(30) Attitude towards Problem Solving

Confidence: I am sure that I can do this, and maybe others can also try to do this.

Arrogance: Only I can do this and what others are doing is a waste of effort.

Giving Feedback: It can be in the following ways:

1. "You have failed again this time."
2. "Last time, your score was 10. This time, it is 20, but remember the passing marks are at 33. This time also, you have failed but with an improved score. Better luck next time and a good try."

Mentoring the Juniors

1. "You have to work on this on your own. Please don't waste my time."
2. "This work is your responsibility. I cannot spoon-feed you. I can surely help you, but first, you have to come up with your prototype."

Communication with the Team

1. "Everytime you do work, it fails. You always crib, and you create a problem everywhere."
2. I sincerely suggest you check the output of the work done by you recently. Also, you may want to discuss or take others' feedback. I will be happy to discuss further once

you complete this. In my opinion, you must improve your working style."

Remember

1. "A clear and defined vision helps in defining the direction of an organization."

2. "Personnel help in unleashing the potential of an organization."

3. "Relationships help in uplifting the morale of an organization."

4. "Leadership determines an organization's success."

(31) Follow Your Passion->Bad job advice?

Sai: I told my son, to take up a job, which matches his passion.

Me :Bad advice.

S: Why?

Me: If I leave out may be, top 5% of the so-called geniuses, in general, people confuse between passion & hobby.

General answer is that my passion is "Music', 'Sports'..

I don't know, whether we all knew our passion in our college days.

Sai: What about Steve Jobs, Jeff Bezos....

Me: They have

1. Curiosity

2. Ability to take risks

3. Ready to fail

4. They were very comfortable, being in 'un-comfortable zone'.

Sai: ?

Me: Let's take person A & B.

Both are good at music.

Person A, practice daily for 9 hours daily.

Person B, practices for 6 hours.

Next 3 hours, he spent time with his mentor to take the 'Brutal feedback' about his music & plan for next day accordingly.

So who will succeed in life?

S : Um..

M: Over period of time only, one can force/flesh out skills which you are good at. But this requires a different mindset.

You need to figure out 'What you can offer the world' & not

'What the world can offer you'.

Many times, right jobs contains these things.

1. Creativity

2. Ability to make an Impact

3. Control over work (Many times, we look for job/work, which helps us in un-leasing our creativity, where we feel that we are able to make an impact on society & we want autonomy/control, while doing this.)

But getting a job, which can offer you these, also demands rare skills.

You may have to do some jobs rightly, before you can find out the right job for you.

Passion & hobby get confused. If I add further, I will say that, even people confuse between, job, career & calling. Job is to pay your bills, career is the path towards better work. A calling is an important part of your life & can be a part of your identity.

(32) Return on Risk…The Amazon way

Sai: What is this 'Successful Failure' culture at Amazon.

Me : Amazon has created a culture of risk taking & learning from that.

1. In 1999, Amazon had launched 'Amazon Auction' to compete with eBay. It failed.

   Post that Amazon had created zShops. It was to attract third party sellers to use Amazon store. This also failed. That time, Third party sellers had to list their product separately on Amazon.

   But taking these learnings, Amazon launched 'Amazon Marketplace.

   Now, more than 50% products sold on Amazon platform are from third party.

2. In 2014, Amazon lost more than $170 Million in Fire Phone. This failed but learnings were applied in Amazon Echo hardware & Alexa.

3. **Pay to Quit:** It seems that once a year, Amazon offers it's seniors "Pay to quit". Headline of the offer is 'Please Don't take the offer'. Idea is to encourage all folks to think, what they really want in long run.

4. **Career Choice:** Amazon pays for 95% of the Tuition fee of employee taking courses (even though these courses may not be relevant for Amazon business). Again, this motivates employees to perform well while at amazon (& not lose this "paid for education benefit).

How are you creating a risk taking culture?

(33) Digital Transformation >SPEED... Li-Fi

This is a conversation between Sai and me about the connection of Wi-Fi and Li-Fi as technology and their comparison.

Sai: With 5G coming, we will have good network speed. Me: Yes. But I am also looking at Li-Fi.

Sai: Li-Fi?

Me: Wi-Fi is Wireless Fidelity and Li-Fi is Light Fidelity. Li-Fi is a wireless communication technology, which utilizes light to transmit data between devices. Mr. Haral used this term in 2011. Light from Light-Emitting Diodes (LEDs) is used as a medium to deliver networked, mobile, high-speed communication similar to Wi-Fi. The speed of Li-Fi can be more than 100 Gbps.

Sai: Wow. So, why I do not hear much about this? But there must be some lags or cons?

Me: Yes, there are some disadvantages.

1. Li-Fi can't be used in dim light. So, this limits the location where Li-Fi can be effective as you require a light source.

2. Also, as light can't pass through walls, the Li-Fi range is limited if there are too many big physical objects.

3. Sunlight and other sources of light can interfere with the Li-Fi signal.

Sai: Um... what next?

Me: I wonder if a combination of Wi-Fi and Li-Fi can be arrived at. That will be fantastic.

(34) Work Culture @NETFLIX

I was reading the book "NO RULES RULES" by REED Hastings & Erin MEYER

Some gems from the book:

1. Increase Talent density in your company. By letting go of 'average performance persons', your highly talented team members will have more fun & passion at work.

2. Avoid stack-ranking systems as they create internal competition & discourage collaboration.

3. Ask yourself "Which of my people, if they told me they were leaving for another company, would I fight hard to keep?"

4. In performance reviews, feedback usually goes only one way & comes from the boss. Not good if you want to create candid work environment.

5. A 360 degree report is good way for feedback. Here provide action items & no fluff.

6. Lead with Context : Provide your team members full information about the company & give them freedom to take decisions in their respective areas. In creative company, not trying a new idea is a bigger sin than failure.

7. In companies, where human life is involved or dangerous work is involved (Mining, hospital ICU..), lead by control.

8. If an idea fails, tell employees to sunshine it openly. That is, share with all, the learning from that failure.

(35) Digital–BIG Data

This was a conversation between me and Sai about some of the interesting use cases of Big Data.

Sai: I have heard a lot about big data usage by Netflix, Facebook and Google. Tell me other interesting use cases.

Me: Ok. They are:

1. **Lotus F1 Team:** In Formula One racing, this helps in saving precious split seconds off lap times. During the race, live data from the car (more than 200 sensors attached to the car) is streamed to engineers in the pit lane. Petabytes of data are shared, and the pit crew is ready to help the driver.

2. **ZSL (Zoological Society of London):** We know only about 20% of various species (plants and mammals), which are part of our ecosystem. Here, satellite images from space, LiDAR, tourist photos were used to understand the animal migration pattern and deforestation. This has helped in getting accurate prediction of the variety and volume of various animal species and to arrive at hot spots where conservation efforts can be focused.

3. **John Deere in Agriculture:** They are helping farmers to access data gathered from sensors attached to their machinery (tractors). Also, crowd sourcing of data related to weather, soil and fertilizer usage in farmers' areas is getting done. Now farmers can take correct decisions related to crops.

Data should finally help you in taking action.

Remember

Data should help you in getting information. Information should help you in getting insights.

And those insights should help you in taking action.

Data->Information->Insights->Action

(36) Power of IOT in our personal life

I am sharing my conversation with my friend Sai on these trivial household repair issues that pop up every now and then:

Sai: This Air Conditioner (AC) is not working. Maybe because we use this AC only during summer time and now maintenance is required for it to work again. Do you remember, last year, we had left the AC remote with batteries inside it? Now, this remote is also not working. I wish I had known it earlier and called the technician.

Me: Do you know that IoT can help you in this case? Sai: Really? How?

Me: IoT connects any device with a chip inside it with another device/Internet. The chip in the device helps in processing and providing relevant information to the Internet. It's the same as having an Alexa at home.

Sai: Yes, I have. I didn't know that Alexa has a connection to IoT.

Me: Just think if all those devices are connected to Alexa through Wi-Fi.

Sai: Interesting…

Me: The latest electronic appliances come with 'Smart Chip'

in them. You can connect such appliances to Alexa. This data can be sent on the CLOUD. So, Alexa will pro- actively tell you which device needs maintenance, and which one is consuming extra power. You can do away with remote controls. Alexa, with a smart screen, will help you out here.

(37) Digital Transformation and Creating a Learning Organization

For a true digital transformation, we must focus on improving the work culture in our organizations.

Do you also get these questions from your team members?

1. I am worried about the future of my current work?

2. Which new technology should I learn?

3. Are my current knowledge and skills relevant for future actions?

I do get these questions & suggest my team to concentrate on these skills, to enter and succeed in digital transformational era.

1. Self-Awareness: You should be aware of your strengths, weaknesses, potentials and opportunities around you.

2. Curiosity: You must have a fire in the belly to know the technology and a will to adapt it to your ways of working.

3. Empathy: Keep an empathetic attitude towards everyone, especially towards co-workers. It would be best if you took the entire team along with you on the growth path.

4. Adaptability: This requires a change in mindset.

5. Learn how to 'Learn and Unlearn '. This is the toughest part.

(38) Transformation: ADOPT or ADEPT

Sai: What does 'CC' or 'BCC' in an e-mail mean? Me: 'Carbon Copy' & 'Blind Carbon Copy'

Earlier, when someone had to send a letter to another person, he or she also used to make a carbon copy and give it to a few others who were relevant to that particular communication, especially business letters.

That practice-and acronym - has now bolted upon new things. We still have folders in an email. PowerPoint has slides as it evolved from Slide Projectors.

Sai: Wow! I didn't realize this.

Me: That's the icing on the cake. Technology has become an essential part of our lives. Whenever a new technology is introduced, everyone gets into the details of it. Once it has been adopted, it just goes into your subconscious mind.

Sai:?

Me: For old people, there is still an offline and online world. I will say that I spend 5 hours online. But for young kids, they don't understand what offline means as they have seen the world online only.

We have some more examples of this in overall human evolution.

1. Before electricity was invented, factories were built near rivers so that they could use steam power (with water). The noise level inside the factory was very high due to this.

    Once electricity made its way, existing factory owners got electric machines for efficiency. The noise level was reduced to a significant extent. But that was only an incremental change.

The big change was - the new players were not obliged to build factories near a river or a water body. They started building factories depending on the availability of raw materials and labors. At present, everyone has adopted this model.

2. Unlike today, we used to communicate over a landline some years back. If we had to talk to a friend, we would fix a time so that he or she could wait for the call near the phone. If we had to visit a city where a friend resided, it was a custom to call him or her in advance. And then came the era of pagers which stayed for a few years. Now, things are different with mobile phones in every pocket; we can call our friends or relatives anytime we want; we need not fix the time or date.

3. After computers entered our lives, Computer Department became the new norm in many companies. During college days, we used to get a slot of 1-2 hours, wherein we could use the machine. The laptop was considered to be a luxury back then. On similar lines, surfing on the internet was an activity that we had to plan during the weekend. Now we carry laptops to our office (and not briefcase). You can surf on your mobile while waiting in a queue or shop.

So, what all have you adopted? Is 'digital' still new to you and you have 'Digital' group in your company? It means that your organization has still not fully adopted the digital.

(39) Gazing Into Future

Main points of the report 'Study of Society from 2021-2025'.

Health

1. Post-COVID, many nations had issued smart chip-based identity cards to all their citizens. This was based on their learning in 2020. This helped in contact tracing & identification of patients.

2. In many houses, with smart wearables, we get the daily data of each family member. Also, based on the usage of smart bathrooms & washrooms, we are able to pro-actively alert family members.

Education

1. Students are attending various subjects like Maths, English and Physics through online classes.

2. They are going to schools to learn soft skills and emotional intelligence. There is a big demand for teachers who can help a group of students in understanding empathy and teamwork.

3. The course curriculum has been changed in many universities. Students are encouraged to use various search engines like Google to get information on various topics. Now, they don't have to memorize everything.

4. Personalized courses are offered depending on the strength of each student.

5. Based on sentiment analysis, parents are able to pro-actively help their children when they are stressed out/depressed.

Insurance

1. Post-self-driving cars, the insurance business had initially taken a hit.

2. In various big companies, Insurance cover is taken for big R&D projects. This has helped in changing the mindset of big companies. They are investing heavily in R&D projects. In case of failure of the project, they get the insured amount back.

Banks

1. Many big technology companies have started lending businesses and deposit/CASA business is left with the banks. This was on expected lines. While taking money from the public as a deposit, these companies had to comply with the regulators, hence, they have not shown much interest here.

2. Banks still have branches, though the number is reduced. The first-level service in these branches is provided by robots and chatbots. This has helped the banks in providing contact-less services to their customers. In case robots are not able to resolve issues, a friendly human team is available to provide support.

Sports

1. Various sports persons are taking the help of robots during the training and practice sessions. Usually, we see a Tennis and Badminton player practicing with robots.

Others

1. After successful introduction of self-driving cars in 2021, young population has stopped buying their own cars.

Also, many car-driving teaching schools have closed. As per a survey, more than 60% of the young population don't have a driving license. This has resulted in major changes in various software application (like banking etc.). Earlier, driving license was used as a valid KYC (Know Your customer) document, in these software application, during on-boarding of new customers.

2. In some countries, where Electric vehicles were introduced in 2021, Electric vehicle charging stations are still less. Also, citizens face lot of problems during rainy seasons. As we had observed in 2024, in a prominent city in a developed country got flooded due to heavy rains and there was water clogging. Due to that, electric supply was switched-off for 48 hours. This had impacted the vehicular movements.

3. As life expectancy has increased, there is a big demand for nurses, nannies and caretakers for the elderly population.

4. In 2024, top 5 countries have declared that now they have enough 'expert technicians', who can do troubleshooting & maintenance of all new smart devices (including smart cars, smart home appliances, smart power grid etc.). This is a major milestone as before 2024, lack of expert technicians was hampering the smooth adoption of various 'Smart' Gadgets/Vehicles/Home appliances…

5. Now air-taxis are available for local transport at a very low cost.

CHAPTER 16

FREQUENTLY ASKED QUESTIONS

I came across some frequent questions on digital transformation required in an organization. In this chapter, I have tried to put them together and answer all the common questions. I hope it will clear your doubts about digital transformation.

Q.   **How do I replace my legacy system?**

Ans.   Product and people should not be tied directly. Customers, their habits and preferences will keep changing. For each new tweak, your product should not change. There should be a layer in between. In the same way, for your legacy system, you should put a layer on top of it, which should talk with your customers. You can offer various UI and experience through this top layer. The in-between processing layer should insulate the product layer from people and the interaction layer. As of now, many systems have tied their product layer with that of customer/UI. Various web pages have been built and mobile APPS launched, and these are directly tied with the product layer. You need to put a layer in-between. Once it is done, you can modify the User/

Interaction layer and upgrade the bottom product layer at a different pace.

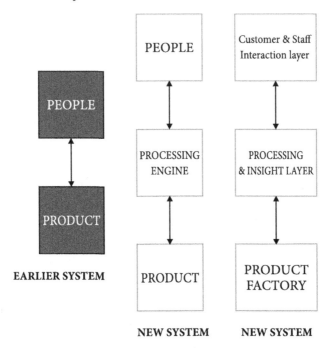

EARLIER SYSTEM   **NEW SYSTEM**   **NEW SYSTEM**

Q.   **How to choose an application if I have to look for a CLOUD-based system?**

Ans. Ask whether that system is built using 12-FACTOR APP. When you are deciding to take any system, make sure that it is built with 12 factors taken into consideration. You will get many vendors, who will claim that their application is on CLOUD. I know many cases where the vendor has just PORTED his earlier application on the Cloud. This won't help. Ask him about these 12 factors; it helps in lowering the TCO (Total Cost of Ownership) of an application.

Make sure that you are not just ticking the box. An application, which truly follows these rules, will be having a lower TCO.

Some of these include:

1. Having all dependencies identified and declared.

2. All configuration parameters stored separately.

3. All applications should produce logs.

4. Having only one code base for different deployment.

5. Self-contained services should talk with other services through agreed and specified ports.

Q. Should I go for micro-services architecture?

Ans. This is a tricky one. Let's first understand how micro-services help. As per the definition, a micro-service helps you to scale only that service, whenever the need arises. For example, let's take an application, which is built to handle both 'Retail and Corporate' customers.

Now, If you are getting too many retail customers, you will definitely want to scale 'the system which is built for Retail customers'. If it is a monolith application (that is both 'Retail & Corporate customer application/functionality are built in together). So 'Retail application' alone can't be scaled up.

So, you end up buying more hardware, provision space, and both Retail and Corporate Application get scaled up.

But remember, you wanted to only scale up Retail application. Hardware bought to scale 'Corporate Customer' is sort of redundant.

In micro-services architecture, you have the flexibility to scale either Retail or Corporate. So can do the scaling properly.

But wait, there is a catch here. Let us assume that the system provider had given you micro-services for Retail and Corporate. What is a logical unit of application which requires to be scaled up? Can't the 'Retail Customer' segment be broken into Small and Medium Retail?

If you really go deep, you will realize that you require too many micro-services... I call them galaxy of stars, and managing all of them can be painful.

While designing microservices, look for:

1. Scalability & Performance attributes of these microservices

2. How easy it is to do the Troubleshooting, Maintenance, Upgrades & Migration of these microservices

3. Whether these microservices are really helping you in quickly/easily compose & roll out new products.

Q.   Why companies are not doing or hesitant to do digital transformation (DT)?

Ans. In my discussions, many times senior management wants to do DT. Many leaders tell me that in fact, they are doing it. Once you get into the details, you will come to know that their company has created a fancy website and launched many mobile apps. They have just provided some more channels through which customers can access their application.

Also, in the majority of cases, the various departments of a company (physical branches vs web application vs mobile apps) do not communicate with each other. This is not transformation. You need to haul the system overall, including the backend, by ACID formula and solve the WISE issues.

An Observation

In many companies, the board comprises of senior managers, who have grown or reached that position by working hard, which was core to that company. For example, in a bank,you will find Chief Risk Officer, Chief Loans Officer or Chief Wealth Investment Officer as senior manager. Many of them would not have got any chance to dabble in technology. The CIO (Chief Information Officer) would take care of necessary IT projects, approved by the business. This work or the project spanned from arranging laptops, getting proper network,buying big machines, including the latest laser printers and other such things. It's very difficult to execute technology-led transformation in an organization where many senior managers don't understand and appreciate the nuances of the technology.

Your company board should consist of 50% technical team members and 50% bankers. Also, if you don't start this transformation in real spirit, even your staff will start moving out. The new generation wants to work and make a difference. If your budget is going towards keeping the lights on (maintaining the old system somehow), the team members will move to other companies.

Q. **So, what is different this time?**

Ans. In a few years, FAAAN companies will start or take away the lucrative part of your business. In banks, you make money through charges and commissions (by providing various services like payment/remittances) and various loans. CASA deposit is not a lucrative thing as banks can be saddled with deposit money, for which they have to pay interest to their customers. If you notice, the lucrative part has already been started to move away from the bank businesses. Various companies are offering loans (from micro to personal). If you are buying a big electronic gadget, that shop/retail store will offer you a loan with an attractive EMI. If you are taking Ola, you can get a loan here as well (that is, you take the taxi ride and pay later). All of these are different forms of loans.

On similar lines, various groups offer payment/money/forex transfer services at a fraction of the cost. Here, it must be noticed the entry barrier to start any business, including banking services, is going down. Yes, to start a bank, you require regulatory approval. But to offer banking services, you just require a good software system, a tie-up with any CLOUD provider and good ideas.

Q. What role does 'Agile' play here?

Ans. IMO, 'Agile & Agility' is more related to mindset. Unfortunately, in many cases, companies had bought various tools and are practicing several rituals (work breakdown, burn-down chart and daily stand-up call), in the name of agility. The mindset has not changed yet.

Let me first give an example from the personal side. Suppose, I have to transfer a huge amount to someone whom I had met for the first time, I'll create the payee through the bank website. Once the payee is registered, I always transfer a small amount say Rs.1,000. Once he confirms receipt of the amount (Rs. 1,000), only then I transfer the rest of the amount.

I could have transferred the full amount the first time, but there is a chance of depositing the money in the wrong account. Now in case, the bank charges me on each transfer transaction, I will not do this. So, I will say that bank has not embraced & encouraged agile mindset. It needs to provide the flexibility of doing money transfers multiple times, freely.

Post that, it is up to me to decide how to complete the transaction.

If someone gives you something new to eat, you would first taste a small portion and then only eat the rest. Even, when you drink hot tea/coffee, you drink sip by sip. On business front also, the same principle applies. First, complete MVP (Minimum Viable Product). This should include product development, testing, implementation and learning by the team. The last part is very important as many times, under pressure, the team just keeps on doing similar work, in the same way. In the case of escalations, the team does RCA (Root Cause Analysis). That RCA tells how the mistake happened. Now, this is a complete waste. You need to learn from those issues and come out with an action plan, which should be implemented in the next cycle. Do small logical things, learn from them and improve the next cycle.

Think of 'Continuous FLOW' of work/services, the flow of logical items, from customer requirements->Product, Build->Testing->Implementation @Customer.

Also, in a truly AGILE world, be ready to accept that your product will always be in a perpetual beta stage. It is based on customer input and the ideas of the team. You have to constantly improve your product. The key is to keep providing more value 'always'. Your relationship with your customers will be a journey. It's not a transaction of the vendor supplying a product and the customer buying it. You have to enhance your value proposition and make sure that in a dynamic changing world, your customers are getting new value, almost daily.

Q. Role of IoT in the service sector, especially the banking or hospitality industry?

Ans. This pandemic (COVID-19) has forced many companies/ industries to re-look at their digital journey and what role physical shops/branches play. This has forced companies to offer their services, anytime, anywhere.

But even in 'new normal', people will visit bank branches. Or for that matter, families are likely to travel and spend a holiday in a hotel or a resort.

Now think of a hotel, where most of the work is automated and can happen without manual touch. Even in the places, where manual work is required, a Robot comes into the picture. At common places, like benches or walls, a smart chip is embedded, which gives an alarm in case it gets infected by a virus. Also, small machines/robots can be placed near these common benches/walls, which dutifully clean up these physical objects, after someone has used them. This can give you the information on how many persons sat on that bench/chair throughout the day and how many times it was cleaned up. Will you be more comfortable going to a resort like this?

The same applies to banks/branches. Most of the branch work can be automated by a robot. Regular cleaning of all devices (printers/scanners/cash dispensers) is also done. Also, a bank branch representative is available to give personal advice.

Q. **How much usage of AI have you seen in banks?**

Ans. To be honest, not much. Many are still in the POC stage.

In live environments, banks are still using AI for (1) Fraud Detection (2) KYC & AML (3) Next Best Product Offer.

There are various use cases through which banks can learn and help customers further. If a customer is buying daily tickets for his official travel, a bank application can review this pattern and suggest the customer buy a monthly pass (which hopefully will be cheaper).

Banks can help/teach their customer's children by allowing the kids to have a wallet. Also, spending from a wallet can be gamified. This will help the kids to become financially literate. Something similar can be done for the elderly parents of the customers as well.

Also, the bank website can have a combination of 'Sand-Box+Useful APP library'. Customers and their families can use this sandbox along with various apps to understand and plan for various complex products,namely, mortgages, margin lending and structured products.

Q. **Apart from the challenges mentioned in the book, what are the other things to watch out for while implementing the digital transformation?**

Ans. Many times, I have observed that the company doesn't go full hog for transformation. It starts to tweak slowly as team members are comfortable with the old processes. Let me give an example here.

A bank starts its automation journey. So, say, earlier some data used to come from outside and a bank official would upload it into the system. For simplicity's sake, let's think that a company sends the salary data, which will be uploaded by the bank and the company employee's account should get credited. This process can be automated. But earlier, the bank official used to check the data, which would come to them. So, even after launching the new system, the bank officials want to control it so that they can review the data. Now, the requirement can be asked due to various reasons. The bank officials are not sure about the accuracy of the file, stability and behavior of the new system. Manual control should be given during the initial period only. But, eventually, people gel with this practice and the purpose of fully automating a system is never achieved.

If you are putting a new system, review and note down:

1. Whether the earlier perceived problem is solved.

2. Telemetry data which tells you really 'what waste got reduced' or 'which new value got generated'.

Leadership plays a key role here. If you look at Adobe's Photoshop, the image editing program, it had achieved cult status. Still, CEO Shantanu Narayen was worried. Apart from various acquisitions, they moved their full offering to a cloud-based subscription business model. This was a tough call as the company was moving away from the perpetual license business model. There was an immediate impact on the next few years' revenues. But this model allowed new customers to start using their offering by paying a small amount ($50 USD per month). And by 2019, Adobe's revenue and stock price zoomed.

Q. **Partner eco-system. What to watch for?**

Ans. Is your product layered? That is, one can buy and implement only one logical component. If needed by the customers, a trusted partner can innovate further on this component. So, remember that your product should be in a state that it can be assembled and used by the 'Plug-and-Play' method. Also, a partner can work on top of this component to provide more value. I call this the extensibility capability of a product.

Q. **Some thought process for banks?**

Ans. Normally in banks, the leader looks for maximum stability and minimum change. But this model has to move to minimum stability and maximum change. A technology company will look at 'Money Management' with lenses of innovation, change and flexibility. On the other hand, the banker will look at technology with lenses of rules, regulations and safety. We have to blend these two. There are various stakeholders like regulators, competitors and investors involved.

We are moving from concepts of "Branch closing to open banking".

The 24-hour banking is here, and hence bank application has to be with the customers all the time. In case a customer is buying a daily ticket for the metro, based on this data, the bank application can suggest him to buy a monthly pass. Financial inclusion can mean that banking is available to everyone. Also, along with the kid's wallet for your customer, a bank can help in cultivating 'good money management' habits in kids from the early days.

Q. **What is Technical Debt? What is the impact of this?**

Ans. In all the software products, technical debt gets accumulated over a period of time. Various reasons are behind it like some product feature being released without full design and test. Some features and codes become redundant over a period of time. As a part of Learning Org, we have to keep an eye on it and make plans to continually reduce this technical debt.

With AI coming into the picture, much more will be added to the debt. In AI, we can create a model and label the input data to improve our code logic. Now, over a period of time, that data will become redundant. This can be due to a variety of reasons, including regulatory changes. The underlying algorithm will keep on getting smarter with various new data & usages.

This again will add to the 'Technical Debt'.

So, we have to re- look and re-factor the model.

REFERENCES

1. The Fifth Discipline book by Peter Senge
2. Creativity, Inc by Amy Wallace and Edwin Catmull
3. Daniel Kahne man's book Thinking, Fast and Slow
4. The Dichotomy of Leadership book by Jocko Willink & Leif Babin
5. Good to Great by Jim Collins
6. No Rules: Netflix and the Culture of Reinvention by Reed Hastings & Erin Meyer
7. The Bezos Letters: 14 Principles to Grow Your Business Like Amazon by Steve Anderson
8. The Infinite Game by Simon Sinek
9. 'Be the business' by Martins heller

Made in the USA
Monee, IL
27 September 2021